B.A.NARASGOUDA.
ADVOCATE

WAYS TO GET DIVORCE, MAINTENANCE OR PERMANENT ALIMONY FROM HUSBAND.

1st Addition

Marriage is an institution by which two people make their relationship public, official, and permanent, and when they both or anyone of them intend to break the relationship publicly, officially and permanently the need for divorce, maintenance and permanent alimony arises.

In order to simply and make understand the law and procedure by which a Hindu woman who is legally married can obtain divorce, permanent alimony or maintenance this book has been published.

With the blessings of " Lord Mahaveer,"

Dedicated to our parents Late Shri Apppasaheb B Narasgouda and Late Smt Sushila Narasgouda.
ABOUT THE BOOK

BHARAT A NARASGOUDA: WAYS TO GET DIVORCE, MAINTENANCE OR PERMANENT ALIMONY FROM HUSBAND.

Publisher's Note

Despite our meticulous care, it is possible that some errors or omissions may have escaped unattended. It may be notified that this publication is being sold on the condition and understanding that information given in this book is merely for reference and must not be taken as having authority of or binding in any way on the authors, editors, printers, publishers and seller who do not owe any responsibility for any damage or loss to any person, or purchaser of this publication or nor, for the result of any action taken on this basis of this work. For Authoritative information, please refer the recent acts, judgments, and Gazette notifications. The Publishers shall be highly obliged if mistakes are brought to their notice for carrying out corrections in next edition.All Disputes will be subject to the exclusive jurisdiction of courts, tribunals, and forums at Karnataka Only.

PREFACE

HINDU MARRIAGE ACT, CRIMINAL PROCEDURE CODE, DOMESTIC VIOLENCE ACT. IPC, DOWRY HARRASSMENT ACT, HINDU GUARDIANS AND WARDS ACT and some more are the most important branches of civil and criminal law governing the Hindu community.

Basically this book is published in order to enlighten the women who are unaware of their rights, and are hesitant to exercise their right knowing very well that the relationship is not working and they intend to come out of relationship, but due to lack of knowledge, fear and other economic problems do not take a step forward to come out of the relationship and waste their life in a meaningless relationship and hence in order to make them aware of law and procedure, which can to some extend help them to make a right decision and lead there life more independently and comfortably this publication has been made.

It is further hoped that the efforts are useful to the readers, Bar and the Bench, Advocates, and the public at large.

GENERAL: Normally Hindu marriages take place as per the customs and ceremonies prevailing in the said society and the law applicable to such marriages performed are governed under the Hindu Marriage Act 1955. The Hindu marriage act is applicable to Hindus only who get married as per the customs and ceremonies prevalent in the society.

Once a Hindu marriage has taken place then the rights and obligations arise, and both are governed under the said law which is Hindu Marriage Act. Further after the Marriage if any party wants that they should come out of the legal relationship then it is through the process of court and the facts and circumstances of each case will decide what must be done. It is to be noted that if any party wants divorce then they must approach the court only other forms of divorce are not recognized. Under the Hindu law, It is often seen in villages that divorce deed is executed on bond paper or some paper and such agreements and divorce deed are not valid and may cause future legal problems so better to approach the court and get a divorce decree which is valid.

INDEX

CHAPTER NO 1.

So the question is when can a woman apply for diverse after marriage and the simple answer to this question is that whenever woman feels that the relationship is not working and she is subjected to domestic violence, cruelty, desertion, husband having extra marital affairs, husband has converted to other religion, or husband is suffering from mental disorder, or suffering from venereal disease in communicable form, or has renounced the world by entering any religious order or has not been heard of as being alive for a period of seven years or more by those persons who would naturally have heard of it had that party been alive or that there has been no resumption of cohabitation as between the husband and wife for a period of one year or upwards after the passing of a decree for judicial separation in a proceeding or that there has been no restitution of conjugal rights as between the parties for a period of one year or upwards after the passing of a decree for restitution of conjugal rights in a proceeding or the husband has been guilty of rape, sodomy or bestiality.

Next question arises as to when can a woman file petition for divorce in the court and the answer to this question a women can file petition only after one year of marriage completion and it is also possible to file a petition before completion of one year of marriage but for that some rules have been framed by concerned high courts and as per section 14 of Hindu marriage Act an application has to be made to the court stating the ground that the case is one of exceptional hardship of exceptional depravity on the part of the respondent and after hearing the application if the court allows the application then the petition for divorce can be filed within 1 year of marriage.

Hence it can be seen that the divorce petition can be filed within one year of marriage only if there are exceptional grounds i.e. if there is some grave reason of exceptional hardship the divorce petition can be filed within 1 year of marriage and if the court is satisfied with the reasons given for applying for divorce within one year of marriage then the court allows the application and then a petition for divorce can be filed within one year of marriage though the court will also make efforts to see that, whether there are any chances of a reconciliation between the husband and wife. Further in respect of mutual consent divorce

there is a condition that the husband and wife must be residing separately for a period of one year or more. Women can apply for permanent alimony under section 25 of the Hindu

marriage Act and she can also apply for interim maintenance and litigation expenses under section 24 of the Hindu marriage Act, wife can also file if petition under section 125 of criminal procedure code and claim monthly maintenance from the husband, further women has an option to file a case of domestic violence in which she can claim maintenance and also get other reliefs as mentioned in the domestic violence act. Wife can you file a petition for divorce and in the same petition she can ask for maintenance as well as permanent alimony from husband. But it is better to file domestic violence or Petition under 125 CRPC to claim maintenance as there is lot of scope for recovery because as far as section 24 of Hindu marriage act is concerned it comes under civil procedure, further it is better that if a women is not able to maintain herself in the standard of living which the husband is enjoying and the women wants a divorce then it is better that a claim for interim maintenance is also made as it has been seen that after passing of the maintenance order by the court the husband comes for compromise and the petition ends with settlement by paying permanent alimony and agreeing for divorce.

CHAPTER NO 2.

Hindu wife can file a petition in the below mentioned four places as described under section 19 of the Hindu marriage Act which as under.

1. Wife can file a petition for divorce in a place where the marriage was solemnized or, example if marriage has taken place at Mumbai then wife can file Petition at Mumbai or;

2. The wife can file a Petition for divorce at the place where the husband is residing at the time of presentation of the petition for divorce, that means at the place where husband is residing. Example if husband is residing at Delhi the wife can also file Petition at Delhi.

3. The Wife can also file a petition at the place where both the husband and wife last resided together, example if husband and wife last resided at Pune then the wife can file a petition in Pune court.

4. A wife can also file a petition in a place where she is residing at the time of presentation of the petition that means, example if the wife is residing at Bengaluru, she can file Petition for divorce and maintenance in Bengaluru

so, the wife has an option of filing divorce petition/maintenance Petition in all the above 4 places and she can conveniently choose a place where she can attend the court without much difficulty. The husband also can file a petition for divorce as mentioned in about places, except one place that is he is not given the right to file petition where he resides as given to wife, if his wife is residing at some other place, if the marriage has taken place at some other place, or they last resided at some other place, the option is given to a wife alone and she can file a petition where she resides but same is not given to husband. The husband can file Petition where he resides only if at that time the wife is residing outside the territories to which this act extends, or the wife has not been heard of as being alive for a period of seven years or more by those who would naturally have heard of her if she were alive.

CHAPTER NO 3.

If a wife wants divorce, then she has to prove at least one ground as mentioned in section 13 of Hindu marriage Act and on basis of which divorce is granted by the court and the grounds are:

1. If the husband had voluntary sexual intercourse with any person other than his spouse ;or

2. If the husband has treated the wife with cruelty after marriage, cruelty may be physical or mental; or

3. Has deserted the wife for a continuous period of not less than two years immediately preceding the presentation of the diverse petition ; or

4. That the husband has been incurably of unsound mind or has been suffering continuously or intermittently from mental disorder of such a kind and to such an extent that the wife cannot reasonably be expected to leave with the husband, mental disorder means mental illness and arrested or incomplete development of mind, psychopathic disorder or any other disorder or disability of mind and includes schizophrenia, psychopathic disorder means persistent disorder are disability of mind whether or not including sub-normality of intelligence which results in abnormally aggressive or seriously irresponsible conduct on the part of the husband and whether or not it requires or is susceptible to medical treatment; or

5.   If husband has been suffering from venereal disease in communicable form ; or

6.   The husband has renounced the world by entering any religious order ; or

7.   Has not been heard of as being alive for a period of seven years or more by those persons who would naturally have heard of it had husband been alive ; or

8.   That there has been no resumption of cohabitation between husband and wife to the marriage for a period of one year or upwards after the passing of a decree for judicial separation in a proceeding to which husband and wife were parties; or

9.   That there has been no restitution of conjugal rights as between husband and wife to the marriage for a period of one year or upwards after the passing of a decree for restitution of conjugal rights in a proceeding to which husband and wife were parties.

Additional Grounds Provided to The Wife for Divorce:

10.   Besides the grounds enumerated above, a wife has been provided four additional grounds of divorce under Section 13(2) of the Hindu Marriage Act, 1955.

These are as follows-

11.   **Pre-Act Polygamous Marriage**

(i) in the case of any marriage solemnized before the commencement of this Act, that the husband had married again before such commencement or that any other wife of the husband married before such commencement was alive at the time of the solemnization of the marriage of the petitioner: Provided that in either case the other wife is alive at the time of the presentation of the petition ;. Such a ground is available if both the marriages are valid marriages & the other wife (2nd wife) should be present at the time of filing of the petition. However, today this ground is no more of practical importance.

12.   Rape, Sodomy or Bestiality

Under this clause, a divorce petition can be presented if the husband has, since the solemnization of the marriage, been guilty of rape, sodomy, or bestiality.

13.   Non-Resumption of Cohabitation After A Decree/Order of Maintenance

If a wife has obtained an order of maintenance in proceedings under **Section 125, Cr.P.C., 1973** or a decree under Section 18, Hindu Adoption & Maintenance Act, 1956 & cohabitation has not been resumed between parties after one year or upwards, then this is a valid ground for suing for divorce.

14.   Repudiation of Marriage

This provision provides a ground for divorce to the wife when the marriage was solemnized before she attained the age of fifteen years, and she has repudiated the marriage, but before the age of eighteen. Such repudiation may be express (written or spoken words) or may be implied from the conduct of the wife (left husband & refused to come back). Moreover, this right (added by the 1976 amendment) has only a retrospective effect i.e. it can be invoked irrespective of the fact that the marriage was solemnized before or after such amendment.

So if wife is able to prove any of the above points then she will be granted divorce by the court and if she fails to prove any one of the above points then the petition filed by her will be dismissed. It is necessary that in order to prove above points all the documentary, oral and circumstantial evidence are produced in the court in systematic manner so that grounds of divorce are very much clear and easy to understand for the Judge and if the presentation, facts and circumstances are pleaded with certainty and presented in a proper manner backed with recent judgments of courts it will not only help the Judge for passing orders with authority in hand but also make your case free flowing to a systematic end.

CHAPTER NO 4.

HOW TO PROVE GROUNDS FOR OBTAINING DI-VORCE.

Firstly in order to get divorce you have to state all the facts clearly and also disclose all the details of the married life to your advocate by providing all the documents relating to your relationship, incidents that have taken place, property details of husband and yourself, income proof, children details, all social media or electronic evidence, communications, photographs, address proof, and anything which will help in proving the grounds of divorce, further the witness who can testify in your favour and any other relevant documents and facts.

The grounds of divorce can be proved by oral, documentary evidence and circumstantial evidence and the grounds on which divorce is granted are as under as per section 13 of Hindu marriage act:

1. **If the husband had voluntary sexual intercourse with any person other than his spouse after marriage**: In case of sexual intercourse with any other women direct proof is difficult to get and one has to rely for proof on circumstantial evidence and the same may be sufficiently proved from which sexual intercourse with other women can be inferred. The burden of proving sexual intercourse in on the person who makes the allegation. The standard of proof is by preponderance of probabilities and not by proving it beyond reasonable doubt. General evidence of the ill- repute of the husband of the lewd company he keeps, or even that he knows the addresses of prostitutes and was seen with doubtful women, would neither prove nor probabilism intercourse, as a general rule it is proved by presumptive proof on based on circumstantial evidence, evidence of non-ac-

cess and birth of children, contracting venereal disease, evidence of visit to houses of ill- repute women, admissions made in previous proceedings, confessions and admissions of the husband, mere suspicion is not sufficient, there must be circumstances amounting to proof that opportunities could be used, such as the association of the husband was so clear that adultery or illegal relationship might reasonably be assumed as the result of any opportunity for its occurrence. voluntary sexual action by a married person with another married or unmarried individual is a ground for divorce under Hindu marriage act. Almost every religion condemns it and treats it as an unpardonable sin. There is a provision in Hindu Marriage Act which says, a petition either by the husband or the wife can be presented before the court alleging that, the other party has, after the solemnization of the marriage, had voluntary sexual inter-course with any person other than his or her spouse. Therefore, having sexual intercourse voluntarily with someone else other than one's spouse is a valid ground for divorce under the Hindu Marriage Act. A single act of voluntary sexual intercourse by a marriage partner with any person other than their spouse is a ground for a decree of divorce under the provisions of the Hindu Marriage Act,1955. The contention that, wife has been living separate from him since June, 1973 and she gave birth to a child on 1st May, 1974 and therefore it must be held that the wife had voluntary sexual intercourse with a third person, proved to be a valid ground for divorce on the satisfaction of several other considerations. Ensure that the act is sexual intercourse. The following are examples of sexual intercourse

1. Admission of adultery by husband.

2. Testimony of witnesses not interested in the matter that they had seen the man or the women

committing sex and other situations.

Messages on WhatsApp, Facebook, even Google Talk etc. social media are now easy evidence permissible in court. In order to gather evidence as proof against your partner's crime of sexual intercourse one can collect evidences including photographs, video, and more. The easiest way to divorce using sexual intercourse by husband with other person is to make the husband who has committed the infidelity to admit to it. It can be hard to gather evidence and prove sexual intercourse if your husband is not prepared to admit it. You can prove sexual intercourse or infidelity through text messages, hotel room bookings, witnesses etc.,

It should be noted that it is not necessary that the sexual relationship with other person be proved beyond reasonable doubt especially in matrimony cases, Additionally, it is necessary to implead the other person with whom your husband had sex as a co-respondent in the Petition, failing which the Petition may get rejected in the court of law. Once, the accused husband is condoned by you for the act of sex by your husband and he does not commit it again, you cannot use the ground as the ground for divorce, if you have condoned his acts.

The courts in India puts burden on the person who is saying that his estranged spouse had sexual intercourse with other women and invoked the provision of section 13 1(i) of the HMA 1955. Though direct evidence is rarely adduced but largely the evidence is circumstantial.

What are the facts that can prove sexual intercourse?

Since circumstantial evidence is the basis of proving sexual intercourse, the circumstance like husband

and her paramour lived in a Hotel for 1 night and no explanation is given by to this effect then sexual intercourse is presumed for this entry in Hotel register, CCTV footage with certificate under section 65B of IT act may be necessary. It is important to make paramour also a party to the suit though no decree can be sought against the paramour. it is important the evidence of witnesses are of equal weightage like A Husband brings his girlfriend to house in absence of wife and take her into bedroom. the witnesses can be grown up children, neighbors, maid etc. These are the circumstances where Sexual intercourse can be presumed. But a mere suspicion that husband was not home whole night is not enough to prove sexual intercourse.

Even if the paramour of the husband writes filthy letter that too also does not come into an ambit of proving sexual intercourse. what amounts to sexual intercourse is in the eyes of a reasonable person? that circumstances are such that a reasonable man would think it such. like husband is living with paramour for more than 7 months . Another thing is merely having flirtatious conversation with a person not his/her husband/wife does not mean they had Sexual intercourse though it can come under mental cruelty which is also a ground for divorce.

Conclusion

The ingredients for proving sexually intercourse with other women are that the facts in which the intimacy is such that in the eyes of the reasonable person, such intimacy is there, credible evidence needs to be produced before the court to prove sexual intercourse and merely on the basis of whims, fancies and suspicion the same cannot be proved. The court also put the burden of proof on the person alleging. Divorce on ground of sexual intercourse with other women is bit difficult to prove but with oral, documentary and help of witnesses who inspire confidence, the said fact can be proved and now a days with the use of all social media technology like what's up, face book, Instagram, hotel bills, testimonies of hotel staff or persons who saw them in compromising position etc. can help in proving the fact that your husband had Sexual intercourse with other women.

2. If the husband has treated the wife with cruelty after marriage, cruelty may be physical or mental.

CRUELTY:

Cruelty has not been defined in the matrimonial laws. The respected court depend on external aid in each case. After verifying various decisions, we can give the meaning of cruelty as such:

1. Cruelty includes physical and mental cruelty.

2. Cruelty is the res geste (the events) that adverse effects on the mental and physical health, social status, and lifestyle of the other party.

In *Shobha Rani v. Madhukar Reddi, [(1988) 1 SCC 105*, while dealing with "**cruelty**" under Section 13(1) (i-a) of the Act, this Court observed that the said provision does not **define** "**cruelty**" and the same could not be **defined**. "**Cruelty**" may be mental or physical, intentional, or unintentional.

In Samar Ghosh V.Jaya Ghosh, *(2007) 4 SCC 511*, Court considered the concept of **cruelty** and referring to Oxford Dictionary **defines** "**cruelty**' as "the quality of being cruel; disposition of inflicting suffering; delight in or indifference to another's pain; merciless-ness; hard-heartedness'. cruelty refers to violent acts. However, a mere quarrel, petty outrageous behavior or differences between the spouses does not come in the ambit of cruelty because this is something that is common in a day to day married life. Conducts that would amount to cruelty should be grave and severe in nature. Grave violence does not always mean phys-ical violence. Though physical violence is an essen-tial factor that constitutes cruelty but apart from that a continuous process of ill-treatment or mental or physical torture to either of the spouse would also amount to cruelty.

CRULETY AS A GROUND FOR DIVORCE:

There is no such exhaustive definition to what all condition would amount to cruelty but if we go through a case of marital abuse, then we can conclude of certain conditions such as:

- The physical violence on the spouse.
- Having affairs or sex with other women even publicly accepting it.
- And in cases where either of the spouses is falsely accused of committing sexual inter-course or having affairs, doubting the charac-ter of wife.
- The constant manifestation of agony, rage with the addition of yelling or abusing at the spouse.
- Demoralizing and restricting the spouse by every means to be an independent individual

and compelling the spouse to be in a marital relationship where the spouse is left with no other option but to depend on the other.

- Not disclosing any fact or incident of an acquired sexually transmitted disease while they are already into marital life. And the list goes on it is not exhaustive and depends on facts and circumstances of each case.

TYPES OF CRUELTY:

Cruelty for the purpose of section 13 (1) (i-a) is to be taken as a behavior by one spouse towards the other, which causes reasonable apprehension in the mind of the latter that it is not safe for him or her to continue the matrimonial relationship with the other. Cruelty in matrimonial life may be of unfounded variety, which can be subtle or brutal. It may be words, gestures or by mere silence, violent or non-violent. It differs among the people of different scenario.

So, cruelty can be categorized into two types:

Physical cruelty

The matrimonial physical violence resulting in cruelty. Any physical violence, bodily injuries, the threat to life, limb and health apparently causing apprehension in the mind of the woman would constitute physical cruelty on the spouse.

Mental cruelty

The conduct of the concerned party should be grave and substantial, and it must be much more serious than the ordinary wear and tear of daily life. A mental cruelty can vary depending upon different matrimonial cases, so it is impossible to have a uniform standard to go by. Some instances illustrative of what defines mental cruelty as described under :

- On consideration of complete matrimonial life of the parties, acute mental pain, agony and suffering as would not make it possible for the parties to live with each other, could come within the broad parameters of mental cruelty.

- On a comprehensive appraisal of the entire matrimonial life of the parties involved, it becomes abundantly clear that a situation is such that the wronged party cannot reasonably be asked to put up with such conduct and continue to live with other party;

- Mere coldness or lack of affection cannot amount to cruelty however frequent rudeness of language, petulance of manner, indifference and neglect may reach such a degree that it makes the married life for the other spouse intolerable.

- Mental cruelty is a state of mind – The feeling of deep anguish, disappointment, frustration in one spouse caused by the conduct of the other over a long period of time may lead to mental cruelty.

- An unrelenting course of abusive and humiliating treatment calculated to torture, discommode, or render miserable the life of one spouse.

· Sustained unjustifiable conduct and behaviour of one spouse actually affecting physical and mental health of the other spouse – The treatment complained of and the resultant danger or apprehension must be very grave, substantial, and weighty.

· Sustained reprehensible conduct, studied neglect, indifference, or total departure from the normal standard of conjugal kindness causing injury to mental health or deriving sadistic pleasure can also amount to mental cruelty.

· The conduct must be much more than jealousy, selfishness, possessiveness, which causes unhappiness and dissatisfaction. Emotional upset may not be a valid ground for granting a divorce on the grounds of mental cruelty.

· Mere trivial irritations, quarrels, normal wear, and tear of the married life which happens in day to day life is also not an adequate for granting a divorce on the grounds of mental cruelty.

· The married life should be reviewed as a whole and a few isolated instances over a period of years will not amount to cruelty – The ill-conduct must be persistent for a fairly lengthy period, where the relationship has deteriorated to an extent that because of the acts and behaviour of a spouse, the wronged party finds it extremely difficult to live with the other party any longer. This may amount to mental cruelty.

· If a husband submits himself for an operation of sterilization without medical reasons and without the consent or knowledge of his wife and similarly, if the wife undergoes vasectomy or abortion without medical reason or without the consent or knowledge of her husband, such an act of the spouse may lead to mental cruelty;

. Unilateral decision of refusal to have intercourse for considerable periods of time without there being any physical incapacity or valid reason may amount to mental cruelty.

. Unilateral decisions made by either husband or wife after marriage to not have child from the marriage may amount to cruelty.

. Where there has been a long period of continuous separation, it may fairly be concluded that the matrimonial bond is beyond repair – The marriage becomes a fiction though supported by a legal tie – By refusing to sever that tie, the law in such cases, does not serve the sanctity of marriage. On the contrary, it shows scant regard for the feelings and emotions of the parties involved – In such situations, it may lead to mental cruelty, ascertaining mental cruelty is kind of more challenging than proving physical cruelty. Apart from the physical harm if any woman is inflicted with any kind of mental stress or must compromise her mental peace for her spouse or have to constantly go through mental agony, then that amounts to mental cruelty. However, we will never come to know about the psychology of an individual and sometimes people are hypersensitive in nature so in that case if someone accuses someone of having exhibited cruelty then it cannot be entirely true. Therefore, the person will not be entitled to ask for a divorce on grounds of cruelty. Mental strain can happen in various ways so there are no specific criteria which would amount to mental cruelty.

Mental cruelty is a state of mind and feeling with one of the spouses due to the behavior or behavioral pattern by the other. Unlike the case of physical cruelty, mental cruelty is difficult to establish by direct evidence. It is necessarily a matter of inference to be drawn from the facts and circumstances of the case.

An unrelenting course of abusive and humiliating treatment calculated to torture, discommode, or render miserable the life of one spouse. A feeling of anguish, disappointment, and frustration in one spouse caused by the conduct of the other can only be appreciated on assessing the attending facts and circumstances in which the two partners of matrimonial life have been living. The inference has to be drawn from the attending facts and circumstances taken cumulatively. In case of mental cruelty, it will not be a correct approach to take an instance of misbehaving in isolation and then pose the question whether such behavior is sufficient by itself to cause mental cruelty. The approach should be to take the cumulative effect of the facts and circumstances emerging from the evidence on record and then draw a fair inference whether the petitioner in the divorce petition has been subjected to mental cruelty due to conduct of the other.

In ***A. Jayachandra vs. Aneel Kaur (2005) 2 SCC 22,*** the court observed as under:

"the expression 'cruelty' has not been defined in the Hindu Marriage Act. Cruelty can be physical or mental. Cruelty which is a ground for dissolution of marriage may be defined as willful and unjustifiable conduct of such character to cause danger to life, limb or health, bodily or mental, or as to give rise to a reasonable apprehension of such danger. The question of mental has to be considered in the light of the norms of marital ties of the particular society to which the parties belong, their social values, status, environment in which they live. Cruelty, as noted above, includes mental cruelty, which falls within purview of a matrimonial wrong. Cruelty need not be physical. If from the conduct of the spouse, same is established and/or an inference can be legitimately drawn that the treatment of the spouse is such that it causes an apprehension in the mind of the other spouse, about his or her mental welfare then this conduct of cruelty".

Mental cruelty is a state of mind and feeling with one of the spouses due to the behavior or behavioral pattern by the other. The parties are not expected to be an ideal husband and wife; their conduct has to be ascertained in the backdrop of their social status, educational qualifications, physical and mental conditions, and cultural and social background. When a party approaches the Court for seeking the relief of divorce on the ground of cruelty, he or she is expected to give particulars of the facts which according to him, are of such a nature which would have caused mental cruelty to him of such an intensity that made it impossible for him to continue in the relationship. It is not sufficient to merely plead that the respondent had treated the appellant with cruelty. The behavior and conduct should be so acute and grave that it has the effect of causing anguish, disappointment and frustration to the wronged spouse and make it difficult for that spouse to continue with the matrimonial alliance. Adopting the said criteria, the court is expected to assess as to whether the facts pleaded and proved would constitute cruelty sufficient to severe the matrimonial relationship. Every person has his/her own mental makeup — His/her behavior is guided by social status, education, physical and mental condition — General incompatibilities arising from such factors might cause anguish or disappointment to spouse but they are not by themselves cruelty in law — Erring spouse's conduct, in order to constitute mental cruelty, should be of such a nature that it is reasonably not possible to live with him/her — Spouse seeking divorce must give specific details and also furnish proof, from which court may be able to draw an inference that it is impossible to live with erring spouse .

•   Reasons for seeking divorce must be grave and weighty in order to consider mental cruelty the social status of the parties, their customs and traditions, educational level and the environment, in which they have been living will have to be looked into. The Court will have to draw inference and decide on the basis of the probabilities of the case having regard to the effect on the mind of the spouse. The Hon'ble Apex Court in the judgments reported in (2002) 2 SCC 296 [G.V.N.KAMESWARA RAO v. G.JABILLI] and (2005) 2 SCC 22 [A.JAYACHANDRA v. ANEEL KAUR] have taken the view that cruelty will have to be seen by applying the above said principles.

There cannot be any specific definition mental cruelty. The mental cruelty cannot be put in a strict-jacket formula. The concept of mental cruelty cannot remain static. Therefore, no uniform standard can be laid down and Courts will have to prudent and have a practical approach in adjudicating a case based upon its own facts. A sustained course of abusive and humiliating treatment rendering the life of spouse is one of the factums to decide the mental cruelty. However, mere trivial irritations, quarrels, normal wear, and tear of the married life would not amount to mental cruelty. If by the continued ill conduct of a spouse, the relationship deteriorates then such an action alone amounts to mental cruelty. The Hon'ble Supreme judgment in SAMAR CHOSH v. JAYA GHOSH (2007 (3) ALT 62) has observed as follows:- Human mind is extremely complex and human behavior is equally complicated. Similarly, human ingenuity has no bounds, therefore, to assimilate the entire human behavior in our definition is almost impossible. What is cruelty in one case may not amount to cruelty in other case. The concept of cruelty differs person to person depending upon his upbringing, level of sensitivity, educational, family, and cultural background, financial position, social status, customs, traditions, religious beliefs, human values, and their value system. Apart from this, the concept of mental cruelty cannot remain static. It is bound to change with the passage of time, impact of modern culture through print and electronic media and value system etc. what may be mental cruelty now may not remain a mental cruelty after a passage of time or vice versa. There can never be any strict-jacket formula or fixed parameters for determining mental cruelty in matrimonial matters. The prudent and appropriate way to adjudicate the case would be to evaluate it on its peculiar facts and circumstances while taking aforementioned factors in consideration. No uniform standard can ever be laid down for guidance.

Cruelty may be in the form of physical as well as mental by the act either of the husband or the wife. Though, it is the women who have always been subjected to be tortured and harassed by the husband and relatives. Cruelty is the main ground to seek divorce as defined under 'Sec 13(1) (i-a)' of 'The Hindu Marriage Act, 1955' and party who is filing a case must prove that living between husband and wife became impossible due to the cruelty caused by the other.

CONCLUSION:

While dealing with allegation of cruelty as a ground for divorce the courts should have in their mind that the petitioner has to prove that the respondent had behaved in such a way that the petitioner cannot reasonably be expected to live with the other. In construing such behavior to be cruelty within the ambit of Section 13 of the Hindu Marriage Act, the courts will have to look into each and every case having regard to the facts and circumstances of that case. Social status and educational level of the parties, the society they move in, the possibility or otherwise of the parties ever living together and all other relevant facts and circumstances will also have to be seen. In very exceptional cases divorce may be granted on mere accusations and allegations but regard must be had to the context in which they have been made. Absence of Intention should not make any difference in the case, if by ordinary sense in human affairs, the act complained of, could otherwise be regarded as Cruelty. At last we can conclude that anybody can reach the court for the divorce on basis of cruelty, but, the case will be decided by the mere facts of that case, court can extend or summarize the meaning of cruelty according to their own interpretation but within the boundary of the law and without being prejudiced.

DESERTION GROUND FOR DIVORCE

3. : **The husband deserted the wife for a continuous period of not less than two years immediately preceding the presentation of the Divorce petition.** Desertion is also ground for divorce in India, but the most difficult part is how to prove desertion in court of law. A layman may think desertion as his/her spouse is living separately for the period of 2 years that is it. But actually, what courts in India require are the 4 things which are to be established by the spouse who is seeking divorce on this ground of desertion.

1. Animus deserendi-This means the intention to desert, if husband or wife decides to leave the martial co habitation as they does not want to continue with martial obligations or may be called husband/wife under the eyes of the society this means they have developed animus deserendi, once this intention is formed this fulfills one criteria for proving desertion.

   Now this intention can be from both sides or may be a constructive animus deserendi, In constructive animus deserendi when one of the spouse asks the other spouse to leave the house or leave him/her that is constructive animus deserendi, other form is that the a spouse can leave the other spouse with his/her own will that is willful desertion. in both the situation the affected spouse i.e. the spouse which was made to leave in the case of constructive animus deserendi or the spouse which was left alone can pursue the proceeding for divorce if other requirements are satisfied.

2. Separation - Now the Animus deserendi is followed by actual separation, now this separation can be physical or mental one, normally it's the physical one here the actual action takes place merely forming an intention or telling a spouse that I will leave you is not suffice. if it is not followed by some action. Merely an action without the intention is also not suffice both intentions

> to leave and followed by
> action is mandatory in prov-
> ing desertion. Sometime
> there is first physical separ-
> ation and then followed by
> intention and sometimes
> its vice versa, both should
> take place for a continuous
> period of 2 years.

3. Spouse sits mutely while the other spouse has deserted. efforts should be made to render reconciliation, here contact with parents, mother father or other relatives are essential. reconciliation at its own level at first and then involvement of relative is essential, there should be reasonable just cause to leave- There should not be any reasonable cause available to the spouse who is leaving the matrimonial ties, generally cruelty is alleged by defending spouse to defeat the proceedings of desertion in such cases the burden is on the defending spouse to prove cruelty by examining witnesses and medical examinations etc. But if defending spouse fails to prove any of the just causes then this ingredient stand proved.

4. Without the consent- if the deserting spouse does not consent such desertion this final ingredient also stands proved, but how to prove this ingredient? now let us suppose a spouse leaves then there must be continuous efforts from the other side to bring back the spouse, it should not be the case where the other satisfy the court that deserted spouse never consented for such a desertion.

Proving all the aforementioned ingredients are essential to prove desertion in court, if any one element is missing divorce cannot be granted. Generally, cases fall short in 3rd and 4th ingredient. merely living separately even willfully does not guarantee divorce to deserting partner.

Before we proceed to discuss the evidence on record. it is necessary to notice the law governing the desertion as a ground for divorce. STATUTORY PROVISION

Section 13 of Hindu Marriage Act, 1955 Act deals with divorce. It reads as under:

"13. Divorce. (1) Any marriage solemnized, whether before or after the commencement of this Act, may, on a petition presented by either the husband or the wife, be dissolved by a decree of divorce on the ground that the other party (1) (ib) has deserted the petitioner for a continuous period of not less than two years immediately preceding the presentation of the petition:"

Explanation to said section 13 defines what 'desertion' means. It reads as under:

"Explanation In this sub-section, the expression "desertion" means the desertion of the petitioner by the other party to the marriage without reasonable cause and without the consent or against the wish of such party, and includes the wilful neglect of the petitioner by the other party to the marriage, and its grammatical retractions and cognate expressions shall be construed accordingly."

Bipinchandra Jaisinghbai Shah Vs. Prabhavati {AIR 1957 SC 176}, history and development of a concept of "desertion" as a cause of action for grant of decree of divorce has been spelt out. Quoting English authors and Halsbury's Laws of England, the Supreme Court observed thus in para-10:-

"(10) What is desertion? "Rayden on Divorce" which is a standard work on the subject at p.128 (6th Edn.) has summarized the case-law on the subject in these terms:- "Desertion is the separation of one spouse from the other, with an intention on the part of the deserting spouse of bringing cohabitation permanently to an end without reasonable cause and without the consent of the other spouse; but the physical act of departure by one spouse does not necessarily make that spouse the deserting party". The legal position has been admirably summarized in paras 453 and 454 at pp. 241 to 243 of Halsbury's Laws of England (3rd Edn.), Vol.12, in the following words:-

"In its essence desertion means the intentional permanent forsaking and abandonment of one spouse by the other without that other's consent and without reasonable cause. It is a total repudiation of the obligations of marriage. In view of the large variety of circumstances and of modes of life involved, the Court has discouraged attempts at defining desertion, there being no general principle applicable to all cases. Desertion is not the withdrawal from a place but from a state of things, for what the law seeks to enforce is the recognition and discharge of the common obligations of the married state; the state of things may usually be termed, for short, 'the home'. There can be desertion without previous cohabitation by the parties, or without the marriage having been consummated. The person who actually withdraws from cohabitation is not necessarily the deserting party. The fact that a husband makes an allowance to a wife whom he has abandoned is no answer to a charge of desertion. The offence of desertion is a course of conduct which exists independently of its duration, but as a ground for divorce it must exist for a period of at least 2 years immediately preceding the presentation of the petition or where the offence appears as a cross- charge, of the answer. Desertion as a ground of divorce differs from the statutory grounds of adultery and cruelty in that the offence founding the cause of action of desertion is not complete, but is inchoate, until the suit is constituted. Desertion is a continuing offence". The Supreme Court thereafter in the same paragraph held that the quality of permanence is one of the essential elements which differentiates desertion from willful separation. If a spouse abandons the other spouse in a state of temporary passion, for example, anger or disgust, without intending permanently to cease cohabitation, it will not amount to desertion. For the offence of desertion, so far as the deserting spouse is concerned, two essential conditions must be there, namely, (1) the factum of separation, and (2) the intention to bring cohabitation permanently to an end (animus deserendi). Similarly, two elements are essential so far as the deserted spouse is concerned: (1) the absence of consent, and (2) absence of conduct giving reasonable cause to the spouse leaving the matrimonial home to form the necessary intention aforesaid. The petition for divorce bears the burden of proving those elements in the two spouses, respectively. It was further observed that the desertion is a matter of inference to be drawn from the facts and circumstances of each case. The inference may be drawn from certain facts which may not in another case be capable of leading to the same inference; that is to say, the facts have to be viewed as to the purpose which is revealed by those acts or by conduct and expression of intention, both anterior and subsequent to the actual acts of separation. If, in fact, there has been a separation, the essential question always is whether the act could be attributable to an animus deserendi. The offence of desertion commences when the fact of separation and the animus deserendi co-exist. But it is not necessary that they should commence at the same time. The de facto separation may have commenced without the necessary animus or it may be that the separation and the animus deserendi coincide in point of time; for example, when the separating spouse abandons the marital home with the intention, express or implied, of bringing cohabitation permanently to a close. If a deserting spouse takes advantage provided by law and decides to come back to the deserted spouse by a bona fide offer of resuming the matrimonial home with all the implications of marital life, before the statutory period is out or even after the lapse of that period, unless proceedings for divorce have been commenced, desertion comes to an end and if the deserted spouse unreasonably refuses to offer, the latter may be in desertion and not the former. Hence it is necessary that during all the period that there has been a desertion, the deserted spouse must affirm the marriage and be ready and willing to resume married life on such conditions as may be reasonable. It is also well settled that in proceedings for divorce the plaintiff must prove the offence of desertion, like any other matrimonial offence. Hence, though corroboration is not required as an absolute rule of law, the courts insist upon corroborative evidence, unless its absence is accounted for to the satisfaction of the court. At this stage, it is to be noted that while dealing with the issue concerning divorce and marital offence, Lord Goddard, CJ, in the case of Lawson V. Lawson, 1955-1, All ER 341 observed that "These cases are not cases in which corroboration is required as a matter of law. It is required as matter of precaution..." Lachman Utamchand Kirpalani Vs. Meena @ Mota {AIR 1964 SC 40}, the Supreme Court has held that desertion in its essence means the intentional permanent forsaking and abandonment of one spouse by the other without that other's consent and without reasonable cause. 24.In Smt. Rohini Kumari Vs. Narendra Singh {AIR 1972 SC 459}, the Supreme Court yet again held that desertion does not imply only a separate residence and separate living. It is also necessary that there must be a determination to put an end to marital relation and cohabitation. 25.In Geeta Jagdish Mangtant Vs. Jagdish Mangtant {AIR 2005 SC 3508}, the Supreme Court, after narrating the evidence available in the case, held that the conclusion is inevitable, that there was never any attempt on the part of the wife to go to husband's house, therefore, from this fact alone animus deserendi on the part of the wife is clearly established. She has chosen to adopt a course of conduct which proves desertion on her part and that it was without a reasonable cause. Such a course of conduct over a long period indicates total abandonment of marriage. It also amounts to wilful neglect of the husband by the wife. 26.In a more recent judgment in the matter of Malathi Ravi, M.D. Vs. B.V. Ravi, M.D. {(2014) 7 SCC 640}, the Supreme Court has approved its earlier judgment on the point in the matter of Savitri Pandey Vs. Prem Chandra Pandey {(2002) 2 SCC 73} and has reiterated the same view regarding desertion and the nature of proof required in law to establish the marital offence.

4. Husband ceased to be a Hindu is a ground for divorce.

Marriages in the Indian society are not considered as contracts and are considered as the bond between two individuals to share their religious, moral, and social duties and obligations. Divorce is the legal dissolution of marriage so that either of the spouses is free to re-marry someone else after a certain period of time. Divorce is considered as the last resort after giving an opportunity to the spouses to reconcile and resolve their conflicts. Hence if husband ceased to be a Hindu then the wife can file Petition for divorce.

Conversion as a Ground for Divorce

Conversion by one spouse to another religion is a valid ground for the other spouse to file a divorce petition. Conversion here means that the person has voluntarily relinquished his or her religion and adopted another religion after going through some formal ceremony. Hindu Laws On Divorce On Ground Of Conversion, Section 13 of the Hindu Marriage Act lays down various grounds for divorce including adultery, cruelty, desertion, bigamy, incurable unsoundness of mind, conversion or other religion, venereal disease in communicable form, renouncing the world, or has not been heard of for 7 years as being alive and non-resumption of cohabitation for 1 year or more after a decree of judicial separations, or non-restitution of conjugal rights for more than a year after passing of decree of restitution of conjugal rights.

The spouse who ceases to be a Hindu by conversion cannot file a petition for divorce under this section. A contested divorce petition can be filed by the other spouse who has been left by the spouse who has converted. The Hindu laws lay down 2 conditions in which a divorce petition can be filed on the ground of conversion of a spouse. The conditions are as follows:

1. The spouse has ceased to follow the faith of Hinduism and he is no longer a Hindu.

2. The spouse has converted to another religion. Conversion to another religion, however, does not automatically lead to divorce, but it only gives a right to the other spouse to file a petition for divorce under the divorce laws in India.

5. UNSOUND MIND AND MENTAL DISORDER GROUND FOR DIVORCE.

1. That the husband has been incurably of unsound mind or has been suffering continuously or intermittently from mental disorder of such a kind and to such an extent that the wife cannot reasonably be expected to leave with the husband, mental disorder means mental illness and arrested or incomplete development of mind psychopathic disorder or any other disorder or disability of mind and includes schizophrenia, psychopathic disorder means what persistent disorder are disability of mind whether or not including sub-normality of intelligence which results in abnormally aggressive or seriously irresponsible conduct on the part of the husband and whether or not

it requires or is susceptible to medical treatment.

From the language of section 13 (1) (iii) it can be seen that mere abnormal behaviour cannot be a ground for divorce and what is required to be proved by the other spouse is that due to incurable unsoundness of mind of such kind or such an extent that the complainant spouse cannot reasonably be expected to live with him/her. Extremely high degree of proof is required to enable the Court to grant divorce on the ground of unsoundness of mind. Regarding unsoundness of mind as ground for divorce, the Hon'ble Supreme Court had referred to an earlier judgement reported in 3(1988) 4 SCC 247 Ram Narain Gupta Case which reads as follows : The context in which the ideas of unsoundness of 'mind' and 'mental disorder' occur in the section as grounds for dissolution of a marriage, require the assessment of the degree of the 'mental disorder'. Its degree must be such that the spouse seeking relief cannot reasonably be expected to live with the other. All mental abnormalities are not recognised as grounds for grant of decree. If the mere existence of any degree of mental abnormality could justify dissolution of a marriage few marriages would, indeed, survive in law.

Thus, the statute demands two elements to be proved to make a ground of divorce :- (a) Incurable unsoundness of mind and (b) to the extent of which the petitioner cannot be reasonably expected to live with her. mere unsoundness of mind cannot by itself constitute a ground for divorce.

The unsoundness of mind should be to such an extent that it should be incurable that other spouse cannot be reasonably expected to live with the person who is alleged to be mentally unsound. To make a case fall under section 13(1) (iii) it is enough if the petitioner proves that the respondent has been incurably of unsoundness of mind or that the respondent had been suffering continuously or intermittently, a mental disorder of such a kind and to such an extent that the petitioner cannot reasonably be expected to live with the respondent.

Nevertheless, to enable a spouse to obtain matrimonial relief on this ground or any other type of mental ill health, the law (as incorporated in Hindu marriage act) requires that the disease should be of such a quality that the petitioning spouse cannot be reasonably expected to live with the person suffering from the disease. This legislative approach has a rationale. Matrimonial law is concerned with human conduct or human situation, only if, and insofar as, it affects matrimonial happiness. In assessing the effect on matrimonial happiness, the legislature has adopted the test of reasonableness. This keeps the statute free from rigid, mechanical tests. It also leaves the judiciary an element of elasticity which, inter alia, enables the court to adjust the relief according to (i) developments in medical science; (ii) appearance of new or aggravated disease; and unexpected or unusual mental symptoms. The context in which the idea of unsoundness of mind as " mental disorder " occur in matrimonial law as grounds for dissolution of a marriage, requires the assessment of the degree of the " mental disorder". Its degree must be such that the spouse seeking relief cannot reasonably be expected to live with the other. All mental abnormalities are not recognized as grounds for the grant of divorce.

To conclude it is necessary that the oral and documentary evidence supported by the examination and production of a medical expert in the field of mental disorder or unsoundness of mind be produced before the court who can state the mental condition of the husband, hence if the medical expert such as the person who treated or treating the disease or any other medical expert who on examination can state that the said person is suffering from (a) Incurable unsoundness of mind and (b) to the extent of which the petitioner cannot be reasonably expected to live with him then it can prove the ground as mentioned in section 13 (1) (iii) of Hindu marriage act.

It is better to take see if there are any other grounds other than mental disorders as it requires enormous evidence and also expert evidence and all these will consume a lot of time and the relief is dependent on the evidence produced so mental disorder or unsoundness of mind is required to be proved with medical backing, hence if other grounds of divorce are there as per the facts and circumstances of the case better to file a petition on that ground instead of going on the ground of mental disorder or unsoundness of mind.

6. If husband has been suffering from venereal disease in communicable form or.

Venereal disease as stated in section 13 (1) (V) of the Hindu Marriage Act, 1955 means a communicable infection transmitted by sexual intercourse. HIV positive is also a disease transmitted through sex. Having regard to the fact that venereal disease in a communicable form has been mentioned as one of the grounds for divorce, any disease related to venereal disease in a communicable form, will also come under the provision of section 13(1)(v) of the Hindu Marriage Act. Further, the following information about HIV+ was downloaded from Google, which would prove that HIV+ is also related to venereal disease and it is always in a communicable form.

"Acquired immune deficiency syndrome (AIDS) is an infectious disease caused by the human immunodeficiency virus (HIV). There are two variants of the HIV virus, HIV-1 and HIV-2, both of which ultimately cause AIDS.

In order to prove that your husband is suffering from venereal disease in communicable form medical evidence is very much necessary, so it is necessary that an expert doctor is examined in court who can state by examination or medical records that your husband is suffering from venereal disease in communicable form then the court will grant divorce based on the medical evidence produced. At present, it is a ground for divorce if it is communicable by nature irrespective of the period for which the respondent has been suffering from it. The ground is made out, if it is shown that the disease is in communicable form & it is not necessary that it should have been communicated to the petitioner (even if done innocently).

7. The husband has renounced the world by entering any religious order or.

Renunciation of the world" is a ground for divorce under Hindu law, as the renunciation of the world is a typical Hindu notion. Modern codified Hindu law lays down that a spouse may seek divorce if the other party has renounced the world and has entered a holy order. A person who does this is considered as civilly dead. Such renunciation by entering a religious order must be unequivocal & absolute.

8. Has not been heard of as being alive for a period of seven years or more by those persons who would naturally have heard of it had husband been alive.

Under the Act, a person is presumed to be dead, if he/she has not been heard of as being alive for a period of at least seven years. The burden of proof that the whereabouts of the respondent is not known for the requisite period is on the petitioner under all the matrimonial laws. This is a presumption of universal acceptance as it aids proof in cases where it would be extremely difficult if not impossible to prove that fact.

4. That there has been no resumption of cohabitation between husband and wife to the marriage for a period of one year or upwards after the

passing of a decree for judicial separation in a proceeding to which husband and wife were parties.

Either party to the marriage, whether solemnized before or after commencement of the Hindu Marriage Act, 1955 can under Section 10 of the Act file a petition for judicial separation. After a decree is passed in favour of the parties, they are not bound to cohabit with each other. Some matrimonial rights and obligation, however, continue to subsist. They cannot remarry during the period of separation. They are at liberty to live separately from each other. Rights and obligations remain suspended during the period of separation. The grounds for judicial separation are same as for divorce *Under Section 13(1) and (2) of Hindu marriage act*

Judicial separation is a decree, through which either party to the marriage seeks to remove the obligation of co-habitation with the other, not necessarily proving that their marriage has irretrievably broken down. It is a legal way to live separately from the spouse, without obtaining a decree of divorce. Judicial separation does not dissolve the marriage but merely allows you to stay separately while being endured as legally married. Moreover, a decree of judicial separation does not give you the right to remarry.

. Unlike Divorce, Judicial Separation does not require the parties to wait for one year from the time of solemnization of marriage to file the petition. It can be filed any time after the marriage. Under Section 13 of the Hindu marriage act a divorce can be sought on the ground of the judicial separation decree only after it elapses one year, without resumption of cohabitation.

In Judicial Separation proceedings, the court shall pass orders with regards to custody and access to children, the payment of maintenance and lump sums, the transfer of property, the extinguishment of succession rights, etc. Concisely, the power to pass financial orders vests with the court. where a decree of judicial separation has been passed and the parties did not resume their cohabitation even after one year of the passing of such decree, a petition for divorce can be filed. The period of one year shall be calculated from the date of the original order of the trial court. If the parties do not cohabit for a period of one year or upwards after a decree for judicial separation was passed, either party to the marriage can claim dissolution of the marriage. To sum up, a judicial separation is like a "trial divorce" where the couple can live separately for a period of one year. During this period, they can decide whether they are actually hopelessly incompatible as a couple or are just going through a bad phase in their marriage. It gives hope to people that they still have a shot at saving their marriage and avoiding the painful experience of divorce.

- It has been held that unless a case for divorce is made out, the question of granting judicial separation does not arise. Therefore, the Courts while dealing with the applications for judicial separation shall bear in mind the specific grounds raised for grant of relief claimed and insist on strict proof to establish those grounds and shall not grant some relief or the other as a matter of course. Thus, on a petition for divorce, the Court has discretion in respect of the grounds for divorce other than those mentioned in section 13 (1A) and also some other grounds to grant restricted relief of judicial separation instead of divorce straightway

- if it is just having regard to the facts and circumstances.

- Another question that arises is of decree of maintenance vis-à-vis decree for judicial separation. Where a decree for judicial separation was obtained by the husband against her wife who had deserted him, the wife not being of unchaste character nor her conduct being flagrantly vicious, the order of alimony made in favors of the wife was not interfered with by the Court.

Though section 10 of the *Hindu Marriage Act* does not provide any time as to how long judicial separation can last. But section 13 of the Act provides that if there is no resumption of co-habitation between the parties one year after the decree for judicial separation is passed, the parties can get a decree for divorce on this ground itself. But divorce on this ground will be given only when one year has expired after the passing of the decree for judicial separation and not earlier. The reason for this is that one year is a long period and it provides sufficient time to the parties for reconciliation or to arrive at a decision. If the parties fail to overcome their differences within this period, then there is no fun in allowing the legality of the marriage to just linger on when in substance the relationship of marriage has long expired. It is to be noted, however, that if the parties do agree to resume co-habitation any time after the passing of the decree for judicial separation, they can get the decree rescinded by applying to the court. The Act does not refer to any specific grounds on which a decree for judicial separation can be annulled or rescinded. Section 10(2) however, empowers the Court to rescind the decree for **judicial separation** if it considers it just and reasonable to do so. However Courts have repeatedly warned that this power of rescission has to be exercised with great circumspection and not in a hurry and only after satisfying themselves that it would be just and reasonable to allow such rescission, It has been held that unless a case for divorce is made out, the question of granting judicial separation does not arise. Therefore, the Courts while dealing with the applications for judicial separation shall bear in mind the specific grounds raised for grant of relief claimed and insist on strict proof to establish those grounds and shall not grant some relief or the other as a matter of course. Thus on a petition for divorce, the Court has discretion in respect of the grounds for divorce other than those mentioned in section 13 (1A) and also some other grounds to grant restricted relief of judicial separation instead of divorce straightway if it is just having regard to the facts and circumstances. Another question that arises is of decree of maintenance vis-à-vis decree for judicial separation. Where a decree for judicial separation was obtained by the husband against her wife who had deserted him, the wife not being of unchaste character nor her conduct being flagrantly vicious, the order of alimony made in favor of the wife was not interfered with by the Court.

Whilst judicial separation proceedings are rare

compared to those for a divorce, they are an alternative option in cases where there are strong moral objections, cultural reasons or religious beliefs for a party to the marriage not wanting to obtain a divorce.When a decree of judicial separation is obtained, the parties remain married as the decree of judicial separation does not dissolve their marriage (unlike a decree absolute in divorce). Instead, the decree of judicial separation simply relieves the parties of their duty and obligation to live together.

If either party subsequently wishes to end their marriage then a petition for divorce can be filed at a later date and, if a decree of judicial separation has already been granted, the party obtaining it is not prevented from filing a divorce petition on the same or substantially the same facts. This means the fact used in judicial separation proceedings can subsequently be used as proof of a fact in later divorce proceedings.

Furthermore, it is possible for the respondent in judicial separation proceedings to file, in any event, a petition for divorce after he or she has received the other parties' judicial separation petition.

Conclusion: It is better to apply for divorce instead of judicial separation as under section 13A in any proceeding under the act, on a Petition for dissolution of marriage by a decree of divorce, except insofar as the Petition is founded on the grounds mentioned in Clause (ii)(vi) and (vii) of sub section (1) of section 13, the court may, if it considers it just so to do having regard to the circumstances of the case, pass instead a decree for judicial separation. Hence in simple words if you apply for divorce the court may not grant divorce but instead pass a decree for judicial separation is it thinks just so if any party wants divorce and the court passes decree for judicial separation, but there is provision for appeal also or you can wait for one year to lapse and then apply for divorce.

> **15. That there has been no restitution of conjugal rights as between husband and wife to the marriage for a period of one year or upwards after the passing of a decree for restitution of conjugal rights in a proceeding to which husband and wife were parties.**

Section 9: Restitution of conjugal rights: When either the husband or the wife has, without reasonable excuse, withdrawn from the society of the other, the aggrieved party may apply, by petition to the district Court, for restitution of conjugal rights and the Court, on being satisfied of the truth of the statements made in such petition and that there is no legal ground why the application should not be granted, may decree restitution of conjugal rights accordingly.

Explanation–Where a question arises whether there has been reasonable excuse for withdrawal from the society, the burden of proving reasonable excuse shall be on the person who has withdrawn from the society.

What this section merely says is when one person files a petition and obtains a decree for restitution of conjugal rights (i.e. courts orders the other party to join and lead married life) and even after passing of the order if there is no restitution of conjugal rights for a period of one year or upwards then either of them can apply for a decree of divorce on the ground that there has been no restitution of conjugal rights for one year and upwards after passing of the decree for restitution of conjugal rights.

RESTITUTION OF CONJUGAL RIGHTS WHAT LAW IT IS GOVERNED

By a bare reading of the phrase, even a layman can understand that it means "the restoration of the marital rights". But before diving into what the law means, it is important to know what a Conjugal Right essentially is. Under Hindu Law, marriage is considered as the most sacred ceremony. The ceremony of *Saptapadi* in a Hindu marriage imposes certain rights and duties upon both the husband and the wife that they have against each other. These rights and duties which are binding upon both the spouses under Hindu law are termed as Conjugal or Marital rights. Certain important conjugal rights imposed on the spouses are to reside as Husband and Wife under the same roof, Procreation, raising a family etc.

Parties to a marriage have great aspirations for their married life but many times things do not work, and the parties have to go for a divorce. But divorce is a dire step which ends the relation in its totality therefore when one of the spouses feels that there could be a chance to save their relation, he/she can file an application for Restitution of Conjugal Rights to have a new start of their marital relationship. An important note to be made here is that this restitution could be sought for only in the case of a valid marriage.

A decree of restitution of conjugal rights means that the respondent spouse is ordered to cohabit with the plaintiff spouse and have to fulfil his/her duty against the other. Under the *Hindu Marriage Act or the Special Marriage Act* restitution is the only remedy which could be availed by a deserted spouse against his/her partner if he/she wants to continue with the marriage. The decree of restitution of conjugal rights can be enforced through coercive measures in the form of attachment of property when the party complained against willfully disobeys the decree.

Provisions for restitution of conjugal rights is given *under Section 9 of the Hindu Marriage Act, 1955, Section 22 of the Special Marriage Act, 1954* and *Order 21, Rules 32 and 33 of the CPC, 1908.* In **Saroj Rani v. Sudarshan Kumar Chadha**, Hon'ble Supreme Court while validating the constitutionality of Section 9 of the Hindu Marriage Act dealing with restitution observed that in cases of restitution of conjugal rights the respondent spouse becomes liable as per court's order should cohabit with the aggrieved petitioner and fulfil his marital obligations. Provision for restitution of Conjugal Rights under the Hindu Marriage Act, 1955 is given under S. 9 whereas under the Special Marriage Act, 1954 it is given under Section 22. The provisions read identically and are as follows – When either of the spouses has, withdrawn from the society of the other without a reasonable reason, the aggrieved party may file a suit to the district court, for restitution of conjugal rights. The court, on being satisfied with the petitioner's arguments in the petition and after confirmation that there is no legal embargo on such claim can decree restitution of conjugal rights. The decree of restitution can only be given in case of a valid marriage.

Requirements to file Petition for restitution of conjugal rights

1. That the respondent has withdrawn from the petitioner's society.

2. That the withdrawal neither has a reasonable reason nor is legal.

3. That there was no other legal ground for the refusal of relief.

4. That the court is satisfied with the petitioner's arguments.

Thus, these four grounds form the basis of a suit for restitution under all personal laws. This was again ratified in the case of **Sushila Bai v. Prem Narayan**, wherein the court gave an order of restitution and confirmed the above essentials as a ground for restitution. The court in the same case also laid down certain situations which could be taken as a defense in a suit of restitution which is as follows –

1. That the respondent can claim a matrimonial relief as against the suit.

2. That the facts show, and it is proven that the petitioner is guilty of misconduct.

3. That due to certain acts or omissions it becomes impossible for the spouses to live together. Thus, under these circumstances, the suit for restitution is vitiated and the court becomes bound to a decree for a Judicial Separation followed by a Divorce.

When the court has to decide whether the withdrawal was made on a reasonable excuse, the burden of proving the reasonability of the excuse is upon the person who has withdrawn from the society or the respondent. But primarily the onus is on the shoulders of the petitioner to prove the wrong done against him. Once he/she proves his/her case, the burden shifts over the respondent to prove the reasonability of his/her excuse.

CAN A WIFE ASK FOR MAINTENANCE IN CASES OF SUITS FOR RESTITUION OF CONJUGAL RIGHTS?

Section 9 of the Hindu Marriage Act, 1955 in addition to provide for the restitution of conjugal rights also provides for an opportunity to the petitioner spouse to seek maintenance under Section 24 and 25 of the acts. It is to be noted here that maintenance under these provisions could be sought for even in cases where the action concerning maintenance is still pending. Therefore, a wife who does not want the disruption of marriage can get maintenance from her husband directly through these provisions even without actual dissolution. It is clear that the restitution of conjugal rights is a matrimonial remedy which is guided by Indian tradition and custom of sanctity and purity of marriage. It is aimed at preserving the marriage and not at disrupting it thus promoting reconciliation and maintenance of the marital bond. It can, therefore, be said that restitution of conjugal rights is a positive remedy because it is aimed at preserving the noble bond of marriage. We extract Sec.13(1A) below:

"13(1A) Either party to a marriage, whether solemnized before or after the commencement of this Act, may also present a petition for the dissolution of the marriage by a decree of divorce on the ground---

(i) that there has been no resumption of cohabitation as between the parties to the marriage for a period of one year or upwards after the passing of a decree for judicial separation in a proceeding to which they were parties; or

(ii) that there has been no restitution of conjugal rights as between the parties to the marriage for a period of one year or upwards after the passing of a decree for restitution of conjugal rights in a proceeding to which they were parties."

The mischief rule must be borne in mind. What was the law prior to the amendment? What mischief did the legislature attempt to abate by introduction of Sec.13(1A) and the deletion of Clauses (viii) and (ix) of Sec.13? First of all, this has to be ascertained correctly before attempting to answer the three questions referred above. Prior to the amendment under Sec.13(1), a claim for divorce under Clauses (viii) and (ix) could have been made by either spouse only on the ground that the other party has failed to comply with the decree for restitution of conjugal rights within the prescribed period after passing the decree. In short, the application could have been filed only by the decree-holder and not by the one who had suffered the decree. The law contemplated a decree for divorce under Clauses (viii) and (ix) only if a party who suffered the decree did not comply with the same. In short, the one who had suffered the decree could not possibly raise any claim for divorce under Sec.13(1) (viii) or (ix). There can be absolutely no doubt about this position of law that prevailed prior to the amendment in 1964. For the fault of the other spouse who did not comply with the decree, the decree-holder spouse was permitted to claim divorce. The decree-holder spouse could not claim divorce under Sec.13(1)(ix) on the ground that he himself had not complied with the decree for restitution. The judgment-debtor spouse could not make such an application for divorce whose so ever fault it be that led to non-compliance. It is in this context that Sec.13(1A) was introduced into the statute book. We have extracted Sec.13(1A) above. It is crystal clear that by the amendment the legislature wanted to permit or enable the one who has suffered the decree for restitution of conjugal rights/judicial separation also to claim a decree for divorce under Sec.13(1A) Fault to failure is the avenue in refined progressive marital law. Search for fault need not always be there and the fact of irretrievable failure of marriage is recognized progressively by law in various systems of jurisprudence as a valid ground for divorce. It would be puerile to contend that the legislature which brought about the amendment in 1964 did not want to take note of this pressing requirement to move from fault to failure as ground for dissolution of marriage. The Indian social ethos had to be borne in mind. The great emphasis which the Indian society gives to the preservation of the institution of marriage had to be borne in mind. In spite of all that, the legislature widened the avenue for divorce on the ground of non-compliance with the decree for restitution of conjugal rights by affording opportunity to claim divorce on that ground not only to a party who had obtained the decree but also to a party who had suffered the decree, provided the decree for restitution had not been complied with for the stipulated period and there has been no resumption of cohabitation within the prescribed period. The spouse claiming divorce under Sec.13(1A)(ii) does not now have to show the fault of the other spouse. He need only show that notwithstanding a binding decree for restitution of conjugal right, the spouses have not resumed cohabitation—who ever be the decree-holder or judgment-debtor and whosoever fault it be that led to the failure to resume cohabitation.

Any attempt to interpret the entitlement of a party to a decree for divorce under Sec.13(1A) cannot be undertaken by a court without being conscious of the social realities and the legislative destinations that persuaded the legislature to bring about an amendment in the form of Sec.13(1A) after deleting Clauses (vii) and (ix) of Sec.13(1) as it originally stood. According to us, there can be no doubt on what is required to be proved to entitle a party for a decree for divorce under Sec.13(1A)(ii). Such party must prove:

(1) That there has been a decree for restitution of conjugal rights; and

(2) That there has been no restitution of conjugal rights between the parties notwithstanding the lapse of a period of one year (it was two years prior to 27-5-1976).

It is quite easy to understand from a plain reading of Sec.13(1A) that the legislature was not concerned about the responsibility for non-compliance of decree for restitution of conjugal rights. Did the court direct restitution? In spite of such decree, where the parties unable to resume cohabitation? If they could not resume cohabitation, notwithstanding the question as to who had obtained the decree and on account of whose fault the restitution did not take place, both spouses were held entitled to the decree for divorce under Sec.13(1A)(ii). That is the legislative scheme undoubtedly.

The learned counsel for the appellant relies on certain observations in precedents to indicate that really Sec.13(1A) was introduced by the 1964 amendment accepting the theory that irretrievable break down of marriage must be recognized as a ground for divorce under certain special circumstances. Our attention has been drawn to the observations of Justice

Chinnappa Reddy who headed the two Judge Bench in Ms.Jorden Diengdeh v. S.S. Chopra(1) A.I.R. 1985 S.C. 935. Their Lordships were considering whether irretrievable break down of marriage need be recognized as a ground for dissolution of marriage. It is in this context have that we find the following observations which convey eloquently that the principle of irretrievable break down of marriage justifying a decree for dissolution is recognized in Sec.13(1A).

"..........We may also notice that irretrievable break down of marriage is yet no ground for dissolution of marriage under the Hindu Marriage Act also, though the principle appears to have been recognized in Sec.13(1A) and Sec.13(B)."

From Ms.Jorden Diengdeh v. S.S. Chopra (1) A.I.R. 1985 S.C. 935 to Naveen Kohli v. Neelu Kohli (3) A.I.R. 2006 S.C. 1675 the Supreme Court has been repeatedly emphasizing the need to reckon irretrievable break down of marriage as an independent valid ground for divorce. It is now well-settled that a decree on that ground alone cannot be granted until and unless the legislature recognizes that to be a valid ground for divorce. But, as stated in Jorden's case (supra), Section 13(1A)(ii) recognizes the principle that irretrievable break down of marriage must be recognized as a sufficient ground for divorce, at least, under the circumstances enumerated under Section 13(1A) (ii). We have no hesitation to agree that Section 13(1A) (ii) recognizes the principle that irretrievable break down of marriage can be recognized as a valid ground for divorce provided it is shown to the satisfaction of the court that in spite of a decree for restitution of conjugal rights, the spouses have not resumed cohabitation within the prescribed period. That is recognized by the legislature as a valid ground for either of the spouses—decree-holder or the judgment-debtor, to seek divorce. We may at the risk of repetition observe that fault is irrelevant when a claim for divorce is raised under Sec.13(1A). Who is the decree-holder or judgment-debtor in the proceedings for restitution of conjugal rights is also irrelevant? What is relevant is only whether a marriage remains without restitution even after elapse of a period of one year from the date of the decree for restitution. Such dead marriages, the legislature accepts must be put an end to legally. This we hold is the only way to understand Sec.13(1A)(ii) which was introduced by amendment.

A dispute has been raised as to whether Sec.13(1A) is also guided by Sec.23(1)(a) of the Act. There can be no controversy on that aspect now. It is well-settled and trite now that Sec.23(1)(a) controls and guides Sec.13(1A) also. Notwithstanding the fact that the grounds for divorce under Sec.13(1A) have been established, the petitioner claiming a decree for divorce has further got to show that his claim for relief is not barred under Sec.23(1)(a). The position is too well-settled now to require reference to the precedents. The decision in Hirachand Srinivas Mangaonkar v. Sunanda (4) (2001) 4 S.C.C. 125 removes the last trace of doubt, if any, on this question. If a spouse claiming divorce under Sec.13(1A) is found to be guilty of any wrong falling within the sweep of Sec.23(1)(a), notwithstanding the establishment of the ground for divorce under Sec.13(1A), such party shall not be entitled for divorce not because of the ground under Sec.13(1A) has not been established but because relief would be barred under Sec.23(1)(a) of the Act.

We may straightaway extract Sec.23(1)(a) of the Act:

"23. Decree in proceedings.---(1) In any proceeding under this Act, whether defended or not, if the court is satisfied that----

(a) any of the grounds for granting relief exists and the petitioner except in cases where the relief is sought by him on the ground specified in sub-clause (a), sub-clause (b) of sub-clause (c) of clause (ii) of section 5 is not in any way taking advantage of his or her own wrong or disability for the purpose of such relief."Sec.23(1)(a) guides and controls all proceedings under the Act except Clauses (a), (b) and (c) of Sec.5(ii). When Sec.13(1A) was introduced no consequent amendment was introduced in Sec.23. Therefore, Sec.23(1)(a) indisputably controls and guides Sec.13(1A) also. It is here that a proper understanding of the concept of 'wrong' or 'disability' under Sec.23(1)(a) becomes crucial and vital. The concept of 'wrong' Sec.23(1)(a) cannot be understood without reference to the nature of the claims. The nature of the right to claim divorce must certainly have an impact in ascertaining what could be a 'wrong' to disentitle a party to claim such relief under Sec.23(1)(a). In short, there cannot be a universal concept of 'wrong' applicable to all claims. The concept of wrong has to be understood and ascertained, conscious of the nature of the right conferred and the claim staked. An improper understanding of the concept of wrong may lead to denial and frustration of the right conferred and the relief claimed. That has got to be zealously avoided.

That takes us to the crucial question as to what can be reckoned as a wrong for the purpose of

Sec.23(1)(a) of the Act in a claim for divorce under Sec.13(A)(ii) of the Act.

At the outset we must note that Sec.13(1A) and Sec.23(1)(a) have to be read harmoniously. A ground recognized under Sec.13(1)(A) cannot definitely operate as a wrong under Sec.23(1)(a). If that be so, we will have to assume that what the legislature has given with the right hand under Sec.13(1A) is withdrawn and taken back by the left hand under Sec.23(1)(a). The ground has to be established. One claiming the relief of divorce under Sec.13(1A) should not be guilty of any such wrong as to disentitle him for the relief under Sec.13(1A). Reading the two sections harmoniously the conclusion is irresistible that a ground under Sec.13(1A) cannot definitely operate as a wrong under Sec.23(1)(a) to justify refusal of the relief under Sec.13(1A). This principle emerges clearly from the language of Sec.13(1A) considered in the background of the amendment by which Sec.13(1)(viii) & (ix) were deleted and Sec.13(1A) was introduced into the statute book.

We shall now consider the four decisions of the Supreme Court to which reference has been made above. In Dharmendra Kumar's case (supra) the wife had obtained a decree for restitution of conjugal rights. She did not take any steps for execution of the decree for restitution of conjugal rights. She applied for divorce under Sec.13(1A). The husband pleaded that she had committed the wrong of not enforcing the decree for restitution of conjugal rights which wrong he contended was sufficient to justify rejection of the claim for divorce under Sec.23(1)(a). The Supreme Court had occasion to consider the law on the point. The decision of a Full Bench of the Delhi High Court in Gajna

Devi v. Purshotam Giri(10) A.I.R. 1977 Delhi 178 was quoted with approval by Their Lordships. We extract below the observations of the Full Bench of the High Court found approval with the Supreme Court:

"Section 23 existed in the statute book prior to the insertion of Section 13(1A)..............Had Parliament intended that a party which is guilty of a matrimonial offence and against which a decree for judicial separation or restitution or conjugal rights had been passed, was in view of Sec.23 of the Act, not entitled to obtain divorce then it would have inserted an exception to Section 13(1A) would practically become redundant as the guilty party could never reap benefit of obtaining divorce, while the innocent party was entitled to obtain it even under the statute as it was before the amendment. Section 23 of the Act, therefore, cannot be construed so as to make the effect of amendment of the law by insertion of Section 13(1A) nugatory.

............the expression 'petitioner is not in any way taking advantage of his or her own wrong' occurring in Cl.(a) of S.23(1) of the Act does not apply to taking advantage of the statutory right to obtain dissolution of marriage which has been conferred on him by Sec.13(1A) ....In such a case, a party is not taking advantage of his own wrong, but of the legal right following upon of the passing of the decree and the failure of the parties to comply with the decree........."

After extracting the above passage, Their Lordships of the Supreme Court went on to observe as follows:

"In our opinion the law has been stated correctly in Ram Kali v. Gopal Das (supra) and Gajna Devi v. Purshotam Girl (A.I.R. 1977 Delhi 178 (supra)."

27. Subsequently in the same paragraph 3 the Supreme Court has summarized the quintessence of the law as to how Sec.13(1A) has to be harmonized with Sec.23(1)(a). The conclusion of the Two Judge Bench of the Supreme Court appears in the following words in paragraph 3:

"Therefore, it would not be very reasonable to think that the relief which is available to the spouse against whom a decree for restitution has been passed should be denied to the one who does not insist on compliance with the decree passed in his or her favour. In order to be 'wrong' within the meaning of Section 23(1)(a), the conduct alleged has to be something more than a mere disinclination to agree to an offer of reunion, it must be misconduct serious enough to justify denial of the relief to which the husband or the wife is otherwise entitled."

We reckoned that as the binding statement of law. The wrong put forward under Sec.23(1)(a) must be "serious enough" to justify the denial of the relief to the petitioning spouse.

Later, in Saroj Rani v. Sudarshan Kumar6 (A.I.R. 1984 S.C. 1562 the Supreme Court had occasion to consider this principle in Dharmendra Kumar's case (supra). That was a case where a consent decree for restitution of conjugal rights was passed in favour of the wife. That decree was not complied with. Of course, there was a dispute as to whether it had actually been complied with or not. The court held that it has not been complied with. The husband applied for divorce under Sec.13(1A). The decree was granted in his favour. A contention was raised that the husband was guilty of a wrong under Sec.23(1)(a) which would justify denial of the relief under Sec.13(1A). It was alleged before the Superior Courts that the husband had suffered the decree for restitution fraudulently. It was under contended that he was guilty of not complying with the decree for restitution even though his wife was willing to comply with the same.

The Two Judge Bench of the Supreme Court considered the question and the crucial observations are available in paragraph 10 which we extract below:

"Counsel for the appellant sought to urge that the expression 'taking advantage of his or her own wrong' in clause (a) in sub-section (1) of Section 23 must be construed in such a manner as would not make the Indian wives suffer at the hands of cunning and dishonest husbands. Firstly, even if there is any scope for accepting this broad argument, it has no factual application to this case and secondly if that is so then it requires a legislation to that effect. We are therefore unable to accept the contention of counsel for the appellant that the conduct of the husband sought to be urged against him could possibly come within the expression 'his own wrong' in Section 23(1)(a) of the Act so as to disentitle him to a decree for divorce to which he is otherwise entitled to as held by the Courts below. Furthermore we reach this conclusion without any mental compunction because it is evident that for whatever be the reasons this marriage has broken down and the parties can no longer live together as husband and wife, if such is the situation it is better to close the chapter."

. In the nature of the legislation that is presently available—in the wake of the language in Sec.13(1A), the ground which is recognized as ground for divorce cannot obviously operate as a wrong under Sec.23(1)(a)..

In one decision the finding recorded by the courts below is that the husband obtained a decree for restitution of conjugal rights not to act in obedience thereof but, on the other hand, to keep the wife deprived of her right to perform her conjugal duties. The wife made a demand of the husband to let her join him, but he refused to allow her to enter the house, rather he drove her away as also her relatives, whoever attempted to rehabilitate the wife. These acts of the husband were positive wrongs amounting to 'misconduct'. Un condonable for the purposes of Section 23(1)(a) of the Hindu Marriage Act. 1955. Hence, he was rightly denied relief under Section 13(1A) of the said Act.

The learned counsel for the respondent places heavy reliance on the decision of the Supreme Court in Hirachand Srinivas Mangaonkar v. Sunanda4 (2001) 4 S.C.C. 125. In that case the wife had obtained an order of judicial separation on the ground of adultery. The spouses were residing separately after the order of judicial separation was passed. There was a direction for payment of alimony. The husband did not pay the amount. He continued his adulterous relationship. As a dutiful husband he did not attempt to resume cohabitation in spite of the decree for judicial separation. After the lapse of the stipulated period under Sec.13(1A), he came to court with a petition for dissolution of marriage under Sec.13(1A). The Supreme Court took the view that in not paying alimony to his wife and child, in continuing the adulterous relationship and in not attempting to resume cohabitation continuing. In spite of the decree for judicial separation, the husband can be held to have committed a wrong within the sweep of Sec.23(1)(a). The Supreme Court had referred to the decision in Dharmendra Kumar's case (supra), though we note that the decision in Saroj Rani's case (supra) has not been specifically referred to. This decision is also rendered by a two Judge Bench of the Supreme Court.

The Supreme Court had only held that after establishment of the ground under Sec.13(1A) it must further be shown that the grant of a relief is not barred under Sec.23(1)(a). Even after concluding that the ground under Sec.13(1)(A) has been established satisfactorily, the courts are obliged to consider whether the claim for relief's barred under Sec.23(1)(a). As to what would constitute a wrong, no straight jacket formula can be prescribed. The totality of inputs have to be taken into account to decide whether a conduct of the petitioner spouse which is relied on by the spouse defending the claim for divorce, can be reckoned as wrong for the purpose of Sec.23(1)(a). Sec.23(1)(a) the court has a discretion to grant relief or not under Sec.13(1A). We repeat that the ground under Sec.13(1A) must be established. Once that is established the court has to proceed to consider whether the claim for the relief for divorce is barred under Sec.23(1)(a). As to what would constitute a wrong, no straight jacket formula can be prescribed. The totality of inputs will have to be considered. At any rate, the mere fact that a spouse who has suffered an order of restitution of conjugal rights had not shown inclination or earnestness to resume cohabitation cannot be reckoned as a wrong under Asec.23(1)(a). Something more serious and more grave must be established to justify the rejection of the claim for divorce by invoking the concept of wrong under Sec.23(1)(a).

CHAPTER 5

PERMANENT ALIMONY & MAINTENANCE UNDER SECTION 25 OF HINDU MARRIAGE ACT

Permanent alimony and maintenance.-

(1) Any court exercising jurisdiction under this Act may, at the time of passing any decree or at any time subsequent thereto, on application made to it for the purpose by either the wife or the husband, as the case may be, order that the respondent shall, while the applicant remains unmarried, pay to the applicant for her or his maintenance and support such gross sum or such monthly or periodical sum for a term not exceed-

ing the life of the applicant as, having regard to the respondent's own income and other property, if any, the income and other property of the applicant and the conduct of the parties, it may seem to the court to be just, and any such payment may be secured, if necessary, by a charge on the immovable property of the respondent.

(2) If the court is satisfied that there is a change in the circumstances of either party at any time after it has made an order under sub-section (1), it may, at the instance of either party, vary, modify or rescind any such order in such manner as the court may deem just.

(3) If the court is satisfied that the party in whose favor an order has been made under this section has remarried or, if such party is the wife, that she has not remained chaste, or, if such party is the husband, that he has had sexual intercourse with any woman outside wedlock, it shall rescind the order.

The law on alimony and maintenance also varies as per personal law. For example, under the Hindu Marriage Act, 1955, both the husband and wife are legally entitled to claim permanent alimony and maintenance. However, if the couple marries under the Special Marriage Act, 1954, only the wife is entitled to claim permanent alimony and maintenance.

ALIMONY UNDER MUTUAL CONSENT DIVORCE

When a couple gets divorced by mutual consent, the decision on whether any alimony/maintenance is to be paid by either party is a matter of agreement between them. In such cases, alimony/maintenance could be paid by either the husband to the wife or by the wife to the husband subject to the mutual understanding between the couple. The court passes the decree of divorce on terms agreed between the couple.

The decree binds the couple and is capable of being enforced by the court.

In contested matters, the court intervenes and decides the issue of permanent alimony/maintenance on the merits of each case. The power of the court to grant alimony is not limited to cases where the decree is obtained by the wife. Courts have powers to grant alimony to the wife even where the husband is granted a decree. It is quite possible there may be no alimony/maintenance awarded at all depending upon the facts and circumstances of the case. Assessment of the amount of permanent alimony is entirely the court's discretion.

The factors that the court takes into consideration for permanent alimony/maintenance for the wife as follows:

1) The status and position of the husband, his income, his assets, and his lifestyle –

The position and status have reference more to the financial than to the social position. Income and financial status are the most important factors while arriving at a justified amount to be awarded as alimony/maintenance.

2) The reasonable wants of the wife - Want is not confined to what is required for keeping the claimant wife alive and providing for food only. When a minor child is living with the mother, the necessities of the child are also considered. Much emphasis is given on the reliefs prayed for by the wife by taking into consideration the status and standard of life of the parties, the duration of the marriage, support and education of children, the ability of the spouse to earn and their future prospects, as also their age, health, liabilities, liabilities of the husband and the reasonable wants of the wife.

3) The wife's own income or earnings –

The court will not only take into account the position of the husband but also the position and situation of the wife. In case the wife is working and drawing a handsome salary, the Court will certainly take that into consideration along with the husband's income and then depending on the facts and circumstances of the case decide whether alimony/maintenance is to be awarded to the wife and if yes, then the amount she shall receive from the husband.

As discussed earlier, under the provisions of the Hindu Marriage Act, 1955, even a Hindu husband can claim alimony from his wife if he earns less than her or does not earn at all, though this is rare. Usually, the husband is bound to maintain his wife till her lifetime.

However, if the wife remarries, the husband is absolved of his responsibility and can petition the court for orders to stop the alimony. Similarly, if there is a change in circumstances, that is, the husband is unable to maintain the wife due to a financial crisis or any other adverse situation and the wife is financially independent earning a decent salary, then the husband may petition to the court to address the changed circumstances. The court may, considering the facts, evidences and circumstances prevailing at that point of time, modify, vary, or rescind the order.

The discretion to award lump-sum alimony or a periodical amount vests with the court. If the spouse paying alimony/maintenance earns more income after the award for permanent alimony/maintenance has been passed in the case then the wife receiving alimony/maintenance may make a petition addressing the court about the increase in the husband's income but she will have to prove her inability to maintain herself with the alimony already awarded by the court. The court may consider the facts, evidences and circumstances prevailing at that point of time increase the alimony payable. However, just because his income goes up does not necessarily mean she will get more alimony.

In the future, if the person receiving alimony gets richer (creates/inherits more wealth) than the one paying, can the flow of alimony be reversed? This would again depend upon the facts and circumstances of the case. In case the wife receiving alimony inherits wealth and becomes richer, then the husband would have to make a miscellaneous petition to prove the same to the court. The court will again look into the merits of the case, that is, evidences produced to show that the wife is a richer lady than what she was when alimony was granted to her, inability of the husband to maintain the wife, and if he claims alimony to be awarded to him, that will again be decided by the court after looking into the parameters for awarding alimony/maintenance as discussed above.

In layman's terms alimony and maintenance is monetary compensation granted to a spouse who is unable to support himself or herself. "The compensation depends on the matrimonial laws specific to specific religions. Or civil laws like the Special Marriage Act 1954 and 125 CrPc Common Social Welfare Law," there are two types of alimony and maintenance "For the sake of understanding we can say that the maintenance amount is given during the time of court proceedings. The second type is given after the legal separation. The former is called interim alimony and maintenance and the latter is called permanent alimony and maintenance. Permanent alimony is a provision that comes into effect upon the dissolution

of the marriage or judicial separation. Here the amount fixed by the court is required to be paid either as a lump sum amount or as a fixed periodic payment. These payments stop upon the death of either of the spouse or a date given by the judge. Under the Hindu Marriage Act 1955, both husband and wife can ask for it. "But it's usually the woman who gets the maintenance from the husband. But there have been cases where the court has ordered the wife to pay maintenance. For instance, in case of husband's physical disability that prevents him from earning,". There is no one fixed formula to decide the amount. There are a number of factors that are considered. "There are various factors like income of both spouses, their standard of living, financial status, net worth, as well as each individual's financial need, that are taken into account,". "Generally, it's 1/3rd to 1/5th gross earnings of the spouse who has to pay when it's a lump sum alimony and not more than 25% of husband's salary as monthly maintenance as per a Supreme Court judgement. If the woman is earning and there is a substantial difference between her net worth and her husband's net worth, she still may be granted alimony for the same living standards as her husband's.

"Alimony does not constitute child support," Maintenance of children has to be provided separately. "The husband is not required to pay in case the wife remarries, though he still is supposed to pay a maintenance amount to support children," Common sense says a lump sum amount is better than a periodic payment. Lump sum gives more certainty, as far as regular fixed pay goes, it can stop after a while in case of the spouse's job loss.

In case the spouse stops or delays payments there is a recourse. "You can approach the court in such a case and petition the court to attach the husband's salary," Here the maintenance amount is deduced by the spouse's employer and given to you before the person is paid the salary. "All kind of jewelry, property and other valuables, including cash, appliances, gadgets, given to the woman at marriage, before marriage or during the course of marriage is part of streedhan. This includes items given from family, relatives, friends, husband, in-laws, and acquaintances. This also includes the woman's earning before or after marriage as well as savings and investments made from her earnings,". Divorce is not easy but knowing your rights and getting what's right fully yours will only made your future life a little bit easier.

It is seen sometimes that the wife is unaware or does not know any details of the husband like in which company he works, what is his salary, his PAN Number, his property details, his Aadhaar card, his assets, his investments, his loans and liabilities, his ancestral properties details his share in such properties, his Business details, GST Number, his bank account details, foreign tours, hotel bills, or any other sources of income which he has, any health issues which she has and medical documents to prove the same, hence if wife does not know the required details this makes it difficult for a women to prove the income of the husband before the court if she does not know the details of her husband, hence if a wife knows the details such as PAN number, GST, his education etc., she can get the income tax returns, or sales returns from the department through court summons, if a women knows the property number she can get the property extracts and record of rights from the revenue department, further if she knows the car Number or vehicle

Number she can get the details of ownership from the transport department through court process or summons, she can also get all his bank details his salary certificate, through court process and prove the same before the court so that the permanent alimony and maintenance can be decided and it makes it easy for the court also to decide the permanent alimony or maintenance. Further if she is suffering from any health issues to produce evidence regarding the same, Further it is also necessary to state her own financial position and difficulties and the amount of permanent alimony and maintenance she requires in order to lead life in the same standard of living as the husband is enjoying. In her application, the wife can specify the kind of lifestyle and status which she enjoyed during her stay with the husband.

SUPREME COURT RULES ON BENCHMARK FOR ALIMONY

The Supreme Court of India in its recent decision[1] held that a benchmark of 25% of the net salary of a husband was held to be a "just and proper" amount as alimony to his former wife.

The Supreme Court noted that the amount of permanent alimony awarded must be befitting the status of the parties and the capacity of the spouse to pay maintenance. It has stated that *"maintenance is always dependent on the factual situation of the case and the court would be justified in moulding the claim for maintenance passed on various factors"*. Section 25 of the HMA confers powers upon the court to grant a permanent alimony to either spouse who claims the same by making an application. The section also confers ample power on the court to vary, modify or discharge any order for permanent alimony or permanent maintenance in the event of "change in the circumstances of the parties". Section 125 of the Code of Criminal Code, 1973, also criminalizes the neglect or refusal of a person to maintain his wife, children, or parents. Alimony (maintenance, support, or sustenance) is the financial support that is provided to a spouse after divorce. Generally, it is provided if a spouse does not have adequate means to take care of the basic needs of life. Although, according to law, alimony can be granted to either spouse, usually, it is required to be awarded by the husband to his wife.

Who is eligible to get alimony?

Under Section 25 of the Hindu Marriage Act, permanent alimony is provided by the court to the wife or even to the husband for her or his support and maintenance. In case the wife is a working woman, but there is a considerable difference between her and her husband's net earnings, she will still be awarded alimony to help her maintain the same standard of living as her husband.

If the wife is not earning, the court will consider her age, educational qualification and ability to earn to decide the amount of alimony. If the husband is disabled and is unable to earn and the wife is earning, then the court grants alimony to the husband.

How is alimony calculated?

There is no fixed formula or hard and fast rule for the calculation of alimony that the husband needs to provide to his wife. The alimony can be provided as a periodical or monthly payment, or as a one-time payment in the form of a lump-sum amount.

If the alimony is being paid on a monthly basis, the Supreme Court of India has set 25% of the husband's net monthly salary as the benchmark amount that should be granted to the wife. There is no such benchmark for one-time settlement, but usually, the amount ranges between 1/5th to 1/3rd of the husband's net worth. That being said, there are certain factors that are taken into consideration by the court while computing the alimony amount. Such factors may be varied and may include the following:

- Husband's and wife's incomes and other properties if any
- Conduct of both the husband and the wife
- Mandatory deductions such as income tax, EMIs, loan repayments etc. are considered to calculate the net income of the husband
- Liabilities of the husband, such as dependent parents
- Social status and lifestyle of both the parties
- Age and health condition of both the parties
- The period for which the couple had been married
- Expenses for education and upbringing of the child/children, hence based on a range of factors, which depend on the specific circumstances and facts of each case, the amount of alimony or sustenance to be granted is decided by the court.

- In respect of the claims of permanent alimony under Section 25 of the Hindu Marriage Act, the Court may direct the parties to file affidavits of their assets, income and expenditure, if the same has not already been filed by the parties.
- Generally it is necessary that along with a divorce petition the relief of permanent alimony

or maintenance should be claimed, it is to be noted that even in the divorce case or judicial separation case filed by husband or wife maintenance can claimed maintenance under section 24 and permanent alimony under section 25 of the Hindu marriage act. In one decision of the court the court said that in respect of the claims of permanent alimony under Section 25 of the Hindu Marriage Act, the Court may direct the parties to file affidavits of their assets, income and expenditure, if the same has not already been filed by the parties so that the order of permanent alimony or maintenance can be passed without much delay.

It is to be noted that if the court is satisfied that there is a change in the circumstances of either party at any time after it has made an order under sub-section (1) of section 25 of permanent alimony or periodical payment, it may, at the instance of either party, vary, modify or rescind any such order in such manner as the court may deem just and further if the court is satisfied that the party in whose favor an order has been made under this section has remarried or, if such party is the wife, that she has not remained chaste, or, if such party is the husband, that he has had sexual intercourse with any woman outside wedlock, it shall rescind the order.

CHAPTER NO. 6

SECTION 24 OF HINDU MARRIAGE ACT interim maintenance and Litigation expenses.

Section 24 of the Hindu Marriage Act empowers the Court to award maintenance pendente lite and litigation expenses to a party who has no independent income sufficient for his/her support in proceedings pending under the Hindu Marriage Act, 1955, having regard to the income of the parties. The Proviso to Section 24 provides that application under Section 24 shall be disposed of within 60 days of the date of service of notice on the opposite party.

• If the disposal of maintenance application is taking time and the delay is causing hardship, ad-interim maintenance be granted to the claimant spouse on the basis of admitted income of the respondent.

INTERIM Maintenance & LITIGATION EXPENSES- It is also referred to as maintenance **pendente lite** which is awarded by the courts during the continuation of proceedings of the divorce. The purpose is to meet the necessary and immediate expenses of the spouse who is a party to the proceedings. On satisfaction, the court may grant it. Section 24 of **Hindu**

Marriage Act,1955 deals with this kind of maintenance. Further interim maintenance can be claimed under *Section 125* of **CrPC also.**

Under *Section 24* of the act if the court considers fit and is satisfied that either wife or husband does not have an independent income, then it can order the respondent to pay the maintenance to the petitioner in accordance with the provisions of this Section. Thus, the claimant can be a husband as well. S. 24 - Is a manner of providing maintenance in a summary manner to a party who has no independent income sufficient for her or his support and intended to ensure that at the litigation, both parties are at par. S. 24 - Maintenance pendente lite and litigation expenses can be granted during pendency of any matrimonial proceedings under the Act irrespective of whether the marriage between the parties was valid or void - For example, if a petition under Section 11 of the Act is filed alleging that marriage between the parties was void, during pendency of such petition, maintenance pendente lite can be awarded under Section 24 of the Act, even if subsequently the petition is allowed and marriage between the parties is held to be null and void. S. 24 - Maintenance of child - Act being an enactment that deals with matrimonial issues between the spouse ought to therefore make possible a claim for maintenance of not merely of the spouses but also of children and further a maintenance for spouse at all times ought to be understood as including a claim to maintenance for the child as well, for after all a child is never a party or is not even considered to be a party. S. 24 - Mere fact that husband has burdened to maintain his new wife, child and parents is no ground to decline the legal right of respondent-wife to get maintenance pendente lite under Section 24 of the Hindu Marriage Act, as she has no independent sufficient income to maintain herself. Hindu Marriage Act, 1955 (25 of 1955) S. 24 - Protection of Women from Domestic Violence Act, 2005 (43 of 2005) - When maintenance is awarded under two different Acts, the Court is required to take into consideration all the facts including the right of the applicant-wife, minor children and shelter i.e. rent for having a roof over the head of the concerned party - Amount paid by the petitioner-husband to the respondent-wife towards her maintenance under the provisions of the Domestic Violence Act is required to be adjusted against the amount payable under Section 24 of the 1955 Act. That respondent is not entitled to claim maintenance pendente lite owing to proceedings under Section 125 Cr.P.C., is erroneous - Right is conferred under the specific Section of the HMA and is in the nature of statutory right -Proceedings under Section 125 Cr.P.C. are generally initiated by wife with the hope and expectation that she would get quick and speedier relief in those proceedings by way of maintenance for herself and the child - Initiation of proceedings under Section 125 Cr.P.C. and Section 24 of the HMA, at the best, can be said to be two different modes for maintenance which are statutorily conferred under the HMA - Criminal Procedure Code, (II of 1973) S. 125. In addition to Section 24, the Court is also empowered to pass interim orders in terms of Section 26 of the Act with regard to custody, maintenance, and education of minor children. Maintenance covers not merely food, clothing, and shelter, but also includes other necessities. The quantum and type of necessities covered within the scope of maintenance may vary, depending on the status, financial position and number of dependents, etc. and is at the discretion of the court, Under the Hindu Marriage Act, 1955, there are two types of maintenance—interim or temporary, and permanent—that can be ordered by a court. The former, under Section 24, is the maintenance granted to a spouse during the pendency of court proceedings, while the latter includes permanent maintenance and alimony under Section 25. The maintenance does not include stridhan, which is the wife's right. According to a Supreme Court ruling, even if an estranged wife is earning, she can make a claim for maintenance if her income is not sufficient to sustain her. So, the belief that a working woman cannot claim maintenance does not hold true. Various Acts, such as the Code of Criminal Procedure, 1973, also ensure that the woman can demand maintenance even if she is separated and not divorced. Besides, as per a high court ruling, a husband cannot get away with not paying maintenance to his wife by saying that he is jobless or is not earning. Maintenance is not charity, which is given by the husband to the wife. It is the duty of the husband to see that the wife does not starve and thereby become incapable to prosecute the appeal."

"Subsistence is a bare need and the husband during pendency of the appeal cannot escape from that responsibility," the object of Section 24 of the Act is to ensure that a party to a proceeding does not suffer during pendency of the proceeding by reason of poverty. An order passed under section 24 of the Hindu marriage Act, 1955 awarding maintenance pendente lite and litigation expenses to the spouse can be enforced by resorting to execution proceedings as provided under section 28 A of the act where you can get the salary attached, property attached etc as per section 28 A. The other remedy available in law to enforce order of maintenance is by taking more drastic means like stay of trial/dismissal of petition, adjournment sine die and even dismissal of appeal of defaulting party, striking off defence etc.

An interim maintenance application can be filed in the any proceeding under the act either by husband or wife under section 24 along with affidavit and other required documents to prove the income of the opposite side and after hearing both the parties the court can grant interim maintenance and litigation expenses, further ex-parte interim maintenance also can be granted if application is filed for the same, ex-parte in the sense that in the absence of other party the court can grant interim maintenance which is subject to review after other party files objection and the matter is heard and decided again based on the facts and circumstances the court can vary, cancel or modify the order passed as it seems just.

CHAPTER NO 7

SECTION 26 OF HINDU MARRIAGE ACT

Custody of children.

In any proceeding under this Act, the court may, from time to time, pass such interim orders and make such provisions in the decree as it may deem just and proper with respect to the custody, maintenance and education of minor children, consistently with their wishes, wherever possible, and may, after the decree, upon application by petition for the purpose, make from time to time, all such orders and provisions with respect to the custody, maintenance and education of such children as might have been made by such decree or interim orders in case the proceeding for obtaining such decree were still pending, and the court may also from time to time revoke, suspend or vary any such orders and provisions previously made: [58] [Provided that the application with respect to the maintenance and education of the minor children, pending the proceeding for obtaining such decree, shall, as far as possible, be disposed of within sixty days from the date of service of notice on the respondent.

Under Section 26 of the Act, the court has been empowered to pass any order or make any arrangement in respect of custody, maintenance and education of children during the pendency of the proceedings or after any decree is passed under the Act in any case between the parents of the children. In the absence of any such proceeding only the Guardian Courts can pass such order.

The Act makes provision only in respect of minor children. The orders made under the section can be varied, suspended, or revoked from time to time and even after the termination of the proceedings. The object of the section is to enable the court to make just and proper provision for the welfare of minor children.

Though the section contemplates for entrustment of the child taking into consideration the wishes of the child, in this case, it is the welfare of the child that must be taken into consideration, and the order passed under Section 26 extracted above is only an interim relief. The court can also revoke, suspend, or vary its order from time to time. It is further said that while considering an application under Section 26 of the Hindu Marriage Act, the provisions therein also shall be looked into, and the court is given complete jurisdiction whenever a marriage is dissolved or a judicial separation is made. At any rate, it is the duty of the court to take into consideration the welfare of the child, which is of paramount importance.

In considering the question of custody of a minor while exercising jurisdiction under Hindu Marriage Act, Section 26 alone should be looked at, as it gives complete jurisdiction to the court whenever a marriage is dissolved or an order for judicial separation is made and it becomes the duty of the court to take into consideration the welfare of the child which is of paramount importance. The court should not be influenced by the fact of remarriage as all other considerations must be subordinate to the paramount consideration of the welfare of the minor.

While taking into consideration the welfare of the minor, even though the court is guided only by Section 23 of the Hindu Marriage Act in passing the order, certain statutory provisions are also relevant in this connection. Under the Hindu Minority and Guardianship Act, Section 6(a) deals as to who are the natural guardians of a Hindu minor. It says thus:

The natural guardians of a Hindu minor, in respect of the minor's person as well as in respect of the minor's property (excluding his or her undivided interest in joint family property), are (a) in the case of a boy or unmarried girl the father, and after him, the mother, provided that the custody of a minor who has not completed the age of five years shall ordinarily be with the mother.

Why I am emphasizing the Proviso is that the Statute recognizes the presumption that a child of tender age must be in the custody of the mother, and that alone will be good for the welfare of the child. Even though it is only a recognition by the Statute, all along that was the presumption.

Proviso to Clause (a) of the section lays down that ordinarily the custody of children of tender years will be with the mother. The tender age is considered up to the age of five years. This is a mandatory provision, qualified by the word 'ordinarily. ' The rationale of this provision is that since father is the guardian of all his children a special provision for child of tender years is needed. It is mandatory in the sense that up to the age of five the child must be committed to the custody of the mother. Obviously the mother is the only person who can take care of a child of tender years, mother is a suitable person to take charge of the child it is quite impossible to find an adequate substitute for her for the custody of a child of tender years. The custody of a child of tender years, whose interest should be the paramount consideration must be with the mother. It is the mother who could have the interest of the minor upper most at heart, the tender years of the child needing the care, protection and guidance of the most interested person, the mother has come to be preferred to others. Affection, love, and sympathy which the child requires cannot he given by the father in the same measure as can be given by the mother, especially when the child is aged only about two years or little more. where the child was about five years old, the 'prima facie rule which is now quite settled is that, other things being equal, children of the tender age should be with their mother, and where a court gives custody of a child of this tender age to the father it is incumbent on it to make sure that there are really sufficient reasons to exclude the prima facie rule'.

so long as a child is young enough to need the day-to-day care of his or her mother, it is better to leave the child with the mother, it is better to leave the child with the mother unless mother is entirely unsuitable person. The welfare principle', the child's welfare is the 'first and paramount consideration' when a court determines a relevant issue and declares that neither parent had a superior claim.

Also, before the court makes a divorce or separation order it must consider the arrangement for the children, treating the child's welfare as paramount but having particular regard for the child's wishes, the parties conduct in relation to the child's upbringing, the general principle that the child's welfare will be best served by having regular contact with these with parental responsibility and his family and maintaining as good a relationship with his parents as possible, and any risk to the child attributable to the arrangements for his care.

The child's welfare is to be treated as the top item in a list of items relevant to the matter in question. The words connote a process whereby, when all the relevant facts, relationships claims and wishes of parents, risks choices and other circumstances are taken into account and weighed the course to be followed will be that which is most in the interests of the child's welfare as that term is now understood.... It is the paramount consideration because it rules upon or determines the course to be followed.

Applying the welfare test requires an individual assessment in each case. Consequently, Precedent has little value, except perhaps to indicate the approaches which currently find favour with the judiciary. In the past, considerable emphasis was given to a number of 'rules of thumb' which, although potentially conflicting, could be used to predict or justify the outcome of a case. Thus, in disputes between parents, young children and girls were generally placed with their mothers while older boys went to their fathers. Unless there were special circumstances it was thought advisable to place siblings together. While considering the question of custody of child, neither of the parents has absolute right of custody, everything depends upon the welfare of the child, and even the statutory right of guardianship is subordinate to the 'welfare principle

Orders relating to custody of children are by their

nature not final, but are interlocutory in nature and subject to modification at any future time upon proof of change of circumstances requiring change of custody but such change in custody must be proved to be in the paramount interests of the child. The principle that the welfare of the child is of paramount consideration and not the right of the parent to have custody. The mere desire of a parent to have his child must be subordinate to the consideration of the welfare of the child and can be effective only if it coincides with the welfare of the child. Hon'ble Supreme court in Mausami Moitra Gangulivs. Jayant Ganguli, (2008) 7 SCC 673 held that:"19. The principles of law in relation to the custody of a minor child are well settled. It is trite that while determining the question as to which parent the care and control of a child should be committed, the first and the paramount consideration is the welfare and interest of the child and not the rights of the parents under a statute. Indubitably, the provisions of law pertaining to the custody of a child contained in either the Guardians and Wards Act, 1890 (Section 17) or the Hindu Minority and Guardianship Act, 1956 (Section 13) also hold out the welfare of the child as a predominant consideration. In fact, no statute, on the subject, can ignore, eschew, or obliterate the vital factor of the welfare of the minor.

The word "welfare" used has to be construed literally and must be taken in its widest sense. The moral and ethical welfare of the child must also weigh with the court as well as its physical wellbeing. Though the provisions of the special statutes which govern the rights of the parents or guardians may be taken into consideration, there is nothing which can stand in the way of the court exercising its parens patriae jurisdiction arising in such cases." Normally if the court grants custody to one spouse then visiting rights are granted to the other spouse by making some type or arrangement as the court deems fit or as per the agreement reached between the parties.

CHAPTER 8

ORDER FOR MAINTENANCE OF WIVES, CHILDREN AND PARENTS 125. Order for maintenance of wives, children, and parents.—

(1) If any person having sufficient means neglects or refuses to maintain— (a) his wife, unable to maintain herself, or

(b) his legitimate or illegitimate minor child, whether married or not, unable to maintain itself, or

(c) his legitimate or illegitimate child (not being a married daughter) who has attained majority, where such child is, by reason of any physical or mental abnormality or injury unable to maintain itself, or

(d) his father or mother, unable to maintain himself or herself,

a Magistrate of the first class may, upon proof of such neglect or refusal, order such person to make a monthly allowance for the maintenance of his wife or such child, father or mother, at such monthly rate as such Magistrate thinks fit and to pay the same to such person as the Magistrate may from time to time direct:

Provided that the Magistrate may order the father of a minor female child referred to in clause (b) to make such allowance, until she attains her majority, if the Magistrate is satisfied that the husband of such minor female child, if married, is not possessed of sufficient means:

[Provided further that the Magistrate may, during the pendency of the proceeding regarding monthly allowance for the maintenance under this sub-section, order such person to make a monthly allowance for the interim maintenance of his wife or such child, father or mother, and the expenses of such proceeding which the Magistrate considers reasonable, and to pay the same to such person as the Magistrate may from time to time direct:

Provided also that an application for the monthly allowance for the interim maintenance and expenses of proceeding under the second proviso shall, as far as possible, be disposed of within sixty days from the date of the service of notice of the application to such person.]

Explanation.—For the purposes of this Chapter,—

(a) "minor" means a person who, under the provisions of the Indian Majority Act, 1875 (9 of 1875) is deemed not to have attained his majority.

(b) "wife" includes a woman who has been divorced by, or has obtained a divorce from, her husband and has not remarried.

[(2) Any such allowance for the maintenance or interim maintenance and expenses of proceeding shall be payable from the date of the order, or, if so ordered, from the date of the application for maintenance or interim maintenance and expenses of proceeding, as the case may be.]

(3) If any person so ordered fails without sufficient cause to comply with the order, any such Magistrate may, for every breach of the order, issued a warrant for levying the amount due in the manner provided for levying fines, and may sentence such person, for the whole or any part of each month's [allowance for the maintenance or the interim maintenance and expenses of proceeding, as the case may be,] remaining unpaid after the execution of the warrant, to imprisonment for a term which may extend to one month or until payment if sooner made:

Provided that no warrant shall be issued for the recovery of any amount due under this section unless application be made to the Court to levy such amount within a period of one year from the date on which it became due:

Provided further that if such person offers to maintain his wife on condition of her living with him, and she refuses to live with him, such Magistrate may consider any grounds of refusal stated by her, and may make an order under this section notwithstanding such offer, if he is satisfied that there is just ground for so doing.

Explanation.—If a husband has contracted marriage with another woman or keeps a mistress, it shall be considered to be just ground for his wife's refusal to live with him.

(4) No wife shall be entitled to receive an 1 [allowance for the maintenance or the interim maintenance and expenses of proceeding, as the case may be,] from her husband under this section if she is living in adultery, or if, without any sufficient reason, she refuses to live with her husband, or if they are living separately by mutual consent.

(5) On proof that any wife in whose favour an order has been made under this section in living in adultery, or that without sufficient reason she refuses to live with her husband, or that they are living separately by mutual consent.

126. Procedure.—(1) Proceedings under section 125 may be taken against any person in any district—

(a) where he is, or

(b) where he or his wife resides, or

(c) where he last resided with his wife, or as the case may be, with the mother of the illegitimate child.

(2) All evidence in such proceedings shall be taken in the presence of the person against whom an order for payment of maintenance is proposed to be made, or, when his personal attendance is dispensed with, in the presence of his pleader, and shall be recorded in the manner prescribed for summons-cases:

Provided that if the Magistrate is satisfied that the person against whom an order for payment of maintenance is proposed to be made is wilfully avoiding service, or wilfully neglecting to attend the Court, the Magistrate may proceed to hear and determine the case ex parte and any order so made may be set aside for good cause shown on an application made within three months from the date thereof subject to such terms including terms as to payment of costs to the opposite party as the Magistrate may think just and proper.

(3) The Court in dealing with applications under section 125 shall have power to make such order as to costs as may be just.

127. Alteration in allowance.—

[(1) On proof of a change in the circumstances of any person, receiving, under section 125 a monthly allowance for the maintenance or interim maintenance, or ordered under the same section to pay a monthly allowance for the maintenance, or interim maintenance, to his wife, child, father or mother, as the case may be, the Magistrate may make such alteration, as he thinks fit, in the allowance for the maintenance or the interim maintenance, as the case may be.]

(2) Where it appears to the Magistrate that, in consequence of any decision of a competent Civil Court, any order made under section 125 should be cancelled or varied, he shall cancel the order or, as the case may be, vary the same accordingly.

(3) Where any order has been made under section 125 in favour of a woman who has been divorced by, or has obtained a divorce from, her husband, the Magistrate shall, if he is satisfied that—

(a) the woman has, after the date of such divorce, remarried, cancel such order as from the date of her remarriage.

(b) the woman has been divorced by her husband and that she has received, whether before or after the date of the said order, the whole of the sum which, under any customary or personal law applicable to the parties, was payable on such divorce, cancel such order,—

(i) in the case where such sum was paid before such

order, from the date on which such order was made:

(ii) in any other case, from the date of expiry of the period, if any, for which maintenance has been actually paid by the husband to the woman.

(c) the woman has obtained a divorce from her husband and that she had voluntarily surrendered her rights to 1 [maintenance or interim maintenance, as the case may be,] after her divorce, cancel the order from the date thereof.

(4) At the time of making any decree for the recovery of any maintenance or dowry by any person, to whom a [monthly allowance for the maintenance and interim maintenance or any of them has been ordered] to be paid under section 125, the Civil Court shall take into account the sum which has been paid to, or recovered by, such person [as monthly allowance for the maintenance and interim maintenance or any of them, as the case may be, in pursuance of] the said order.

128. Enforcement of order of maintenance.—A copy of the order of [maintenance or interim maintenance and expenses of proceedings, as the case may be,] shall be given without payment to the person in whose favour it is made, or to his guardian, if any, or to the person to [whom the allowance for the maintenance or the allowance for the interim maintenance and expenses of proceeding, as the case may be,] is to be paid; and such order may be enforced by any Magistrate in any place where the person against whom it is made may be, on such Magistrate being satisfied as to the identity of the parties and the non-payment of the [allowance, or as the case may be, expenses, due].

Above provision in simple words

Section 125 of Cr.PC deals with "Order for maintenance of wives, children and parents". According to Section 125(1), the following persons can claim and get maintenance:

- Wife from his husband,

- Legitimate or illegitimate minor child from his father,

- Legitimate or illegitimate minor child (physical or mental abnormality) from his father, and

- Father or mother from his son or daughter.

'Wife' it includes even those cases where a man and woman have been living together as husband and wife for a reasonably long period of time. Strict proof of marriage should not be a precondition of maintenance under Section 125 of the Cr.PC.

Essential conditions for granting maintenance

There are some essential conditions which should be fulfilled for claiming and granting maintenance:

1. Husband should have Sufficient means to pay for maintenance.

2. The husband has Neglected or refused to maintain his wife.

3. The wife claiming maintenance must be unable to maintain himself/herself in the same standard of living which her husband is enjoying.

4. Quantum of maintenance depends on the standard of living.

SUFFICIENT MEANS TO MAINTAIN

If any person has sufficient means for maintenance, then it is his duty to maintain his wives, children, and parents. It is necessary that the husband has sufficient means to provide maintenance. In some decisions it has been held that if the husband is able bodied and healthy that he is under the duty to maintain his wife and children he cannot say that he is jobless and does not have any income.

Neglect or refusal to maintain by Husband to maintain his wife and children

Any person neglects or refuses to maintain his wives, children, and parents in mollified intention or in any type of egoistic behavior on the demand for maintenance by them.

The wife who claims maintenance must be unable to maintain herself in the same standard of living as her husband is enjoying.

It is a particularly important condition for granting maintenance that a person who is claiming maintenance must be unable to maintain himself/herself. For example- If a wife is earning well, then she cannot claim maintenance under this Section if she can maintain herself in the same standard of living as her husband. In one case it was held that the wife who is hale and healthy and is sufficiently educated to earn for herself but refuses to earn from own and claim maintenance from her husband will be entitled to claim maintenance but that her refusal to earn under the circumstances would disentitle her to get complete amount of maintenance.

What Quantum of maintenance is granted?

Quantum of maintenance means the amount of maintenance. Quantum of maintenance depends on the standard of living. For example- If any issues raised in a rich family, then demand for maintenance will be more as compared to poor family according to their standard of living in a prior life.

In simple words, the Court should also make sure that whether maintenance granted is justified according to the status of a family or not?

JURISDICTION of Magistrates & FAMILY COURT to deal with maintenance proceedings

If any person neglects or refuses to maintain his wife, children or parents, then a Magistrate of the First Class or Family court as the case may be can order such person to make a monthly allowance for the maintenance of his wife, children or parents, at such monthly rate as such Magistrate thinks fit, and to pay the same to such person as the direction of magistrate.

If a minor female child is unmarried, then the magistrate can order to make such allowance, until she attains her majority. When a proceeding is pending regarding monthly allowance for maintenance, the Magistrate can order such person to make a monthly allowance for the interim maintenance of his wife, children or parents and the expenses of such proceeding which the Magistrate considers reasonable. An application for the monthly allowance for the interim maintenance and expenses of proceeding should be disposed within sixty days from the date of the notice of the application to such person but due to heavy burden the courts take some time longer unless the advocates make insist them regularly.

According to section if a court order for such allowance for maintenance or interim maintenance and expenses of the proceeding, then it should be payable from the date of the order or if so ordered, then it shall be payable from the date of application for maintenance and expenses of proceedings. If any person fails to comply with the order without sufficient cause, then Magistrate can order to issue a warrant for levying the amount with fines. If the person again fails after the execution of the warrant, then the punishment of imprisonment for a term which may extend to one month or until payment of sooner made is awarded.

Section 126 of Cr.PC deals with "Procedure for maintenance". This Section says the following:

- Proceeding under Section 125 may be taken in the following district:

1. Where he is, or

2. Where he or his wife resides, or

3. Where he last resided with his wife or mother of an illegitimate child.

- Evidence to be taken in the presence of a person against whom maintenance is to be ordered.

- If a person is wilfully avoiding summons, then ex-parte evidence is taken in that case.

CHANGE IN ALLOWANCE :

Alteration in allowance means an order to increase, decrease or remove/cancel the allowance which was ordered by the Magistrate under Section 125.

According to section 127 if a magistrate ordered to give allowance for maintenance under Section 125 according to the conditions of parties at that time, but if the present conditions of parties have changed, then he can also order to alter the allowance.

According to section 127, Magistrate shall cancel or revoke any order given under Section 125 by him, if it appears that it should be cancelled in consequences of any decision of the competent Civil Court. For example- If Magistrate has ordered to give allowance to wife after divorce but Civil Court has ordered to live together. Then, Magistrate has to revoke his order which was given under Section 125.

According to section 127 (3) where an order has been made in favour of women under Section 125, then the magistrate can cancel the order in the following case:

1. If a woman is remarried after divorce.

2. If a woman has taken allowance under any personal laws after divorce.

3. If a woman has voluntary leave her right to maintenance.

According to section 127, the Civil Court shall take into account the sum which has been paid to such person as monthly allowance for maintenance and interim maintenance under Section 125 at the time of making any decree for the recovery of any maintenance.

Enforcement of order of maintenance

Section 128 deals with "Enforcement of order of maintenance". According to this Section, the following are the conditions for enforcement of the order of maintenance:

- Copy of order under Section 125 is given to that person free of cost in whose favour it is made. In case the order is in favour of children, then the copy of the order will be given to the guardian of children.

- If any Magistrate has made an order under Section 125, then any Magistrate of India can enforce this order where that person lives who have to give maintenance.

- The Magistrate has to satisfy two conditions before enforcement of order:

1. Identity of parties, and

2. Proof of non-payment of allowances.

Chapter IX of the Code of Criminal Procedure is essential for the protection of the rights of the wife, divorced wife, children, and aged parents. It is made to protect them from unusual livelihood. In this chapter of Cr.PC, there are various provisions given related to maintenance like who is entitled to maintenance, essential conditions for granting maintenance, Procedure of maintenance, Alteration of the previous order, Enforcement of order of maintenance etc. nature of provisions u/s 125 CrPC is social justice legislation.

In ***Badshah Vs. Urmila Badshah Godse & Another, (2014) 1 SCC 188*** Supreme Court said that nature of provisions under section 125 CrPC is social justice legislation. Nature of provisions u/s 125 CrPC is a social justice legislation. Distinct approach should be adopted while dealing with cases u/s 125 CrPC. Nature of proceeding u/s 125 CrPC is civil

In ***Vijay Kumar Prasad Vs. State of Bihar, (2004) 5 SCC 196*** Supreme Court said that nature of proceeding under section 125 CrPC is Civil. The jurisdiction of magistrate under chapter IX Cr PC is not strictly a criminal jurisdiction. Proceeding u/s 125 CrPC is summary in nature and intended to provide speedy remedy to wife. Strict proof of marriage should not be insisted as pre-condition for maintenance u/s 125 CrPC

In ***Chanmuniya Vs. Virender Kumar Singh Kushwaha, JT 2010 (11) SC 132*** Supreme Court said that the court should not insist to produce strict proof of marriage.

Construing the term 'wife' broad and expansive interpretation should be given to term 'wife' to include even those cases where a man and woman have been living together as husband and wife for a reasonably long period of time, strict proof of marriage should not be a pre-condition for maintenance. Live-in-relationship & presumption of marriage u/s 114 Evidence Act

In *Madan Mohan Singh Vs. Rajanikant, AIR 2010 SC 2933* Supreme Court said that long-term Live-in relationship cannot be termed as walk in and walk out. Live-in-relationship between parties if continued for a long time, cannot be termed in as "walk in & walk out" .There is a presumption of marriage between them.

Standard of proof of marriage under section 125 of CRPC

In *Dwarika Prasad Satpathy Vs. Bidyut Prava Dixit, AIR 1999 SC 3348* Supreme Court described the standard proof of marriage under section 125 of CrPC. The validity of the marriage for the purpose of summary proceeding u/s 125 Cr PC is to be determined on the basis of the evidence brought on record by the parties. The standard of proof of marriage in such proceeding is not as strict as is required in a trial of offence 494 of the IPC. If the claimant in proceedings u/s 125 of the code succeeds in showing that she and the respondent have lived together as husband and wife. The court can presume that they are legally wedded spouses, and in such a situation the party who denies the marital status can rebut the presumption. One it is admitted that the marriage procedure was followed then it is no necessary to further probe in to whether the said procedure was complete as per the Hindu rites in the proceedings u/s 125 Cr PC from the evidence which is led if the magistrate is prima facie satisfied with regard to the performance of marriage in proceedings u/s 125Cr PC which are of summary nature, strict proof of performance of essential rites is not required. After not disputing the paternity of the child born few days after marriage and after accepting the fact that marriage ceremony was performed, though not legally perfect as contended, it would hardly lie in the mouth of the husband to contend in proceeding u/s 125 Cr PC that there was no valid marriage as essential rites were not performed at the time of said marriage. The provision u/s 125 Cr PC is not to be utilized for defeating the rights conferred by the Legislature to the destitute women, children or parents who are victims of social environment. Moreover, order passed u/s 125 Cr PC does not finally determine the rights and liabilities of parties and parties can file civil suit to have their status determined.

Woman not lawfully married not to be treated as 'wife' and not entitled to maintenance u/s 125 Cr PC

In **Savitaben Somabhai Bhatiya Vs. State of Gujarat, 2005 Cr LJ 2141 (SC)**, the Supreme Court held that the legislature considered it necessary to include within the scope of Sec. 125 an illegitimate child but it has not done so with respect to woman not lawfully married. As such, however, desirable it may be to take note of the plight of the unfortunate woman, who unwittingly entered into wedlock with a married man the legislative intent being clearly reflected in Sec. 125 of the Cr PC, there is no scope for enlarging its scope by introducing any artificial definition to include woman not lawfully married in the expression 'wife'. This may be an inadequacy in law, which only the legislature can undo. Even if it is true that husband was treating the woman as his wife it is really inconsequential. It is the intention of the legislature which is relevant and not the attitude of the party. The principle of estoppels cannot be pressed into service to defeat the provision of Sec. 125 of the Cr PC. Second wife entitled to maintenance u/s 125 CrPC if the husband had concealed from her the subsistence of his first marriage

In **Badshah Vs. Urmila Badshah Godse and Another, (2014) 1 SCC 188** Supreme Court said that Second wife is entitled to maintenance under section 125 CrPC if the husband had concealed from her the subsistence of his first marriage. Where the husband had duped the second wife by not revealing to her the fact of his earlier marriage, it has been held by the Supreme Court that the husband cannot deny maintenance to his second wife u/s 125 CrPC in such a case and he cannot be permitted to take advantage of his own wrong by raising the contention that such second marriage was entered during the subsistence of his first marriage, being void under the Hindu Marriage Act, 1955, the second wife was not entitled to maintenance as she was not his legally wedded wife. The earlier judgments of the Supreme Court reported in *(i) Yamunabai Anantrao Adhav Vs. Anantrao Shivram Adhav, (1988) 1 SCC 530 and (ii) Savitaben Somabhai Bhatiya Vs. State of Gujarat, (2005) 3 SCC 636* supporting the said contention of the husband would apply only in those circumstances where a woman marries a man with full knowledge of subsistence of his first marriage. Second wife thus having no knowledge of first subsisting marriage is to be treated as legally wedded wife for purposes of claiming maintenance. Bigamous child entitled to maintenance

In *Bakulabai Vs. Gangaram, (1988) SCC 537* the Supreme Court said that Even though bigamous marriage is illegal u/s 11 of the Hindu Marriage Act, 1955 but when after such marriage Hindu male and female are living together for a number of years as husband and wife, the child born as a result of such union acquires legitimate status u/s 16(1) of the above Act and such child is entitled to maintenance u/s 125 Cr PC.

In ***Chaturbhuj Vs. Sita Bai, AIR 2008 SC 530*** Supreme Court said that Where the husband had placed material to show that the wife was earning some income, it has been held by the Hon'ble Supreme Court that it is not sufficient to rule out the application of Sec. 125 CrPC. It has to be established that with the amount she earned, the wife was able to maintain herself. Whether the deserted wife was unable to maintain herself, has to be decided on the basis of the material placed on record. Where the personal income of the wife is insufficient, she can claim maintenance u/s 125 CrPC. The test is whether the wife is in a position to maintain her in the way she was used to in the place of her husband. The factual conclusions of the court that the wife is unable to maintain herself cannot be interfered with in the absence of perversity.

The second wife is entitled to maintenance under Section 125 and the petitioner duped the respondent by hiding the information about his first marriage. He cannot deny his second wife's right to maintenance. The court's decision was based on the following reasons:

- If a man and woman have been living together for a long time even without a valid marriage, the term of valid marriage entitling such woman to maintenance should be drawn and a woman in such a case should be entitled to maintenance under Section 125.

- A false representation was given to respondent 1 that he was single and was competent to enter into a marital tie with respondent 1. The petitioner cannot be allowed to take advantage of his own wrong and deny maintenance to his second wife. For the purpose of Section 125 CrPC, respondent 1 would be treated as the wife of the petitioner.

- The wife was unaware of the first marriage of the husband.

- The purpose of Section 125 is to achieve 'social justice' which is enshrined in the Preamble of the Constitution of India. A woman who is the second wife is also entitled to the right of maintenance under Section 125 when there is sufficient evidence to prove that she was unaware of her husband's previous wedding and the second wedding was performed in accordance with the personal laws.

- Thus, supreme court judgment on maintenance observed that second wife is not entitled to maintenance generally but where she was unaware of husband's first marriage, she is entitled to maintenance under section 125.

CHAPTER 9

MAINTENANCE UNDER DOMESTIC VIOLENCE ACT 2005

THE PROTECTION OF WOMEN FROM DOMESTIC VIOLENCE ACT, 2005 NO. 43 OF 2005 [13th September 2005.] An Act to provide for more effective protection of the rights of women guaranteed under the Constitution who are victims of violence of any kind occurring within the family and for matters connected therewith or incidental thereto.

Normally whatever reliefs and protection a woman needs in domestic relations is provided under the act, except the relief of divorce, restitution of conjugal rights, Judicial separation for which separate proceedings have to be initiated. In domestic relationship it is necessary to see what the law says as to what amounts to domestic violence which is defined in section 3 of domestic violence act. It covers all kinds of violence faced by a woman at her "shared household".Domestic Violence includes causing any harm or injury to the safety, life, health or wellbeing of the aggrieved woman by committing any physical, sexual, verbal or economic abuse. Moreover, it also includes any injury or harm done to the aggrieved woman or her relative with a view to coerce her or any person, to meet unlawful dowry demand. Threats to commit violence are also covered under this definition.

Some definitions are important under this act such as

"2(a). "Aggrieved person" means any woman who is, or has been, in a domestic relationship with the respondent and who alleges to have been subjected to any act of domestic violence by the respondent." Section 2(f)" defines the expression "domestic relationship" as follows:

"2(f). "Domestic relationship" means a relationship between two persons who live or have, at any point of time, lived together in a shared household, when they are related by consanguinity, marriage, or through a relationship in the nature of marriage, adoption or are family members living together as a joint family." Section 2 (q) defines the expression "respondent" as follows:

"2(q). "Respondent" means any adult male person who is, or has been, in a domestic relationship with the aggrieved person and against whom the aggrieved person has sought any relief under this Act:

Provided that an aggrieved wife or female living in a relationship in the nature of a marriage may also file a complaint against a relative of the husband or the male partner." Section 2(s) defines the expression "shared household" and reads as follows:

"2(s). "shared household" means a household where the person aggrieved lives or at any stage has lived in a domestic relationship either singly or along with the respondent and includes such a household whether owned or tenanted either jointly by the aggrieved person and the respondent, or owned or tenanted by either of them in respect of which either the aggrieved person or the respondent or both jointly or singly have any right, title, interest or equity and includes such a household which may belong to the joint family of which the respondent is a member, irrespective of whether the respondent or the aggrieved person has any right, title or interest in the shared household."

SECTION 3. Definition of domestic violence. -For the purposes of this Act, any act, omission, or commission or conduct of the respondent shall constitute domestic violence in case it –

(a) harms or injures or endangers the health, safety, life, limb, or well-being, whether mental or physical, of the aggrieved person or tends to do so and includes causing physical abuse, sexual abuse, verbal and emotional abuse and economic abuse; or

(b) harasses, harms, injures, or endangers the aggrieved person with a view to coerce her or any other person related to her to meet any unlawful demand for any dowry or other property or valuable security; or

(c) has the effect of threatening the aggrieved person or any person related to her by any conduct mentioned in clause (a) or clause (b); or

(d) otherwise injures or causes harm, whether physical or mental, to the aggrieved person.

Explanation I.-For the purposes of this section,- (i) "physical abuse" means any act or conduct which is of such a nature as to cause bodily pain, harm, or danger to life, limb, or health or impair the health or development of the aggrieved person and includes assault, criminal intimidation and criminal force;

(ii) "sexual abuse" includes any conduct of a sexual nature that abuses, humiliates, degrades, or otherwise violates the dignity of woman.

(iii) "verbal and emotional abuse" includes-

(a) insults, ridicule, humiliation, name calling and insults or ridicule specially with regard to not having a child or a male child; and

(b) repeated threats to cause physical pain to any person in whom the aggrieved person is interested.

(iv) "economic abuse" includes-

(a) deprivation of all or any economic or financial resources to which the aggrieved person is entitled under any law or custom whether payable under an order of a court or otherwise or which the aggrieved person requires out of necessity including, but not limited to, household necessities for the aggrieved person and her children, if any, stridhan, property, jointly or separately owned by the aggrieved person, payment of rental related to the shared household and maintenance;

(b) disposal of household effects, any alienation of assets whether movable or immovable, valuables, shares, securities, bonds and the like or other property in which the aggrieved person has an interest or is entitled to use by virtue of the domestic relationship or which may be reasonably required by the aggrieved person or her children or her stridhan or any other property jointly or separately held by the aggrieved person; and

(c) prohibition or restriction to continued access to resources or facilities which the aggrieved person is entitled to use or enjoy by virtue of the domestic relationship including access to the shared household.

Explanation II.-For the purpose of determining whether any act, omission, commission or conduct of the respondent constitutes "domestic violence" under this section, the overall facts and circumstances of the case shall be taken into consideration.

. Section 2(f) refers to five categories of relationship, such as, related by consanguinity, marriage, relationship in the nature of marriage, adoption, family members living together as a joint family, of which we are, in this case, concerned with an alleged relationship in the nature of marriage.

As this book is mainly concerned with maintenance aspect of wife hence more emphasis is given to it.

"Economic Abuse" is depriving the aggrieved woman from all sorts of financial resources to which she is entitled to under any law or custom or legal order or which she requires out of necessity, such as for running the household, taking care of the children etc. It also includes alienation of the movable or immovable assets in which she has interest too, prohibiting the aggrieved woman or putting restriction on her to continue the use of resources or facilities. Courts have also interpreted not giving food to the aggrieved person, interfering with the aggrieved person's ability to get an employment, forcing a woman to leave her job etc. as a form of economic abuse.

The DV Act is applicable to all women, irrespective of their marital status, age or religious beliefs. The broad definition of "domestic violence" under the DV Act protects the rights of women guaranteed to them under the Indian Constitutional, to achieve a violence free home.

IN CASE OF DOMESTIC VIOLENCE WHERE CAN YOU FILE A COMPLAINT

Any person who has reason to believe that an act of domestic violence has been, or is being, or is likely to be committed, may give information about it to the concerned Protection Officer.

Section 4 of the domestic violence act states as under:

4. Information to Protection Officer and exclusion of liability of informant.-(1) Any person who has reason to believe that an act of domestic violence has been, or is being, or is likely to be committed, may give information about it to the concerned Protection Officer.

(2) No liability, civil or criminal, shall be incurred by any person for giving in good faith of information for the purpose of sub-section (1).

The most important sections under which a woman can get protection and monetary reliefs are under section 12, and 17 to 26 which are as under:

Section 12. Application to Magistrate.-(1) An aggrieved person or a Protection Officer or any other person on behalf of the aggrieved person may present an application to the Magistrate seeking one or more reliefs under this Act:

Provided that before passing any order on such application, the Magistrate shall take into consideration any domestic incident report received by him from the Protection Officer or the service provider.

(2) The relief sought for under sub-section (1) may include a relief for issuance of an order for payment of compensation or damages without prejudice to the right of such person to institute a suit for compensation or damages for the injuries caused by the acts of domestic violence committed by the respondent:

Provided that where a decree for any amount as compensation or damages has been passed by any court in favor of the aggrieved person, the amount, if any, paid or payable in pursuance of the order made by the Magistrate under this Act shall be set off against the amount payable under such decree and the decree shall, notwithstanding anything contained in the Code of Civil Procedure, 1908 (5 of 1908), or any other law for the time being in force, be executable for the balance amount, if any, left after such set off.

(3) Every application under sub-section (1) shall be in such form and contain such particulars as may be prescribed or as nearly as possible thereto.

(4) The Magistrate shall fix the first date of hearing, which shall not ordinarily be beyond three days from the date of receipt of the application by the court.

(5) The Magistrate shall Endeavour to dispose of every application made under sub-section (1) within a period of sixty days from the date of its first hearing.

Under this section the aggrieved person or protection officer or any other person on behalf of the aggrieved person may present an application to the Magistrate seeking one or more reliefs including order for payment of compensation or damages without prejudice to the rights of such person to institute a suit for compensation or damages for injuries sustained in the act of domestic violence committed by respondent. While disposing of an application under sub clause (1) the magistrate shall take into consideration any domestic incident report received by him from the protection officer or the service provider.

It further states that where a decree for any amount as compensation or damages has been passed by any court in favour of the aggrieved person, the amount, if any, paid or payable in pursuance of the order made by the Magistrate under this Act shall be set off against the amount payable under such decree and the decree shall, notwithstanding anything contained in the Code of Civil Procedure, 1908 (5 of 1908), or any other law for the time being in force, be executable for the balance amount, if any, left after such set off. Under this section it specifies the format and particulars of the application and also states that the court shall fix the first hearing date ordinarily within 3 days of its receipt by the court and the court shall try to dispose of the application within a period of sixty days from the date of first hearing.

Section 26 of the DV Act provides that any relief available under Sections 18,19,20,21 and 22 may also be sought in any legal proceeding, before a Civil Court, family court or a criminal court, affecting the aggrieved person and the respondent whether such proceeding was initiated before or after the commencement of this Act. Further, any relief referred to above may be sought for in addition to and along with any other reliefs that the aggrieved person may seek in such suit or legal proceeding before a civil or criminal court. Further, if any relief has been obtained by the aggrieved person in any proceedings other than a proceeding under this Act, she shall be bound to inform the Magistrate of the grant of such relief.

A perusal of Domestic violence act shows that it does not create any additional right in favour of wife regarding maintenance. It only enables the Magistrate to pass a maintenance order as per the rights available under existing laws. While, the **Act** specifies the duties and functions of protection officer, police officer, service providers, magistrate, medical facility providers and duties of Government. A husband is supposed to maintain his un-earning spouse out of the income which he earns.

It must be remembered that there is no legal presumption that behind every failed marriage there is either dowry demand or **domestic violence**. Marriages do fail for various other reasons. The difficulty is that real causes of failure of marriage are rarely admitted in Courts. Truth and honesty is becoming a rare commodity, in marriages and in averments made before the Courts.

WHERE CAN A PETITION OR APPLICATION CAN BE FILED UNDER DOMESTIC VIOLENCE ACT.

The said question is answered under section 27 of domestic violence act which is as under:

27. Jurisdiction – (1) The court of Judicial Magistrate of the first class or the Metropolitan Magistrate, as the case may be, within the local limits of which –

(a) the person aggrieved permanently or temporarily resides or carries on business or is employed; or

(b) the respondent resides or carries on business or is employed; or

(c) the cause of action has arisen, shall be the competent court to grant a protection order and other orders under this Act and to try offences under this Act (2) Any order made under this Act shall be enforceable throughout India.

A plain reading of the above provision makes it clear that the petition under the DOMESTIC VIOLENCE ACT can be filed in a court where the "person aggrieved" permanently or temporarily resides or carries on business or is employed. Normally the wife files the Petition in a place where she is residing unless she feels it convenient to file at other places mentioned in section 27 of domestic violence act.

STRIDHAN

Stridhan has been described as saudayika by Sir Gooroodas Banerjee in "Hindu Law of Marriage and Stridhan" which is as follows:-

"First, take the case of property obtained by gift. Gifts of affectionate kindred, which are known by the name of saudayika stridhan, constitute a woman's absolute property, which she has at all times independent power to alienate, and over which her husband has only a qualified right, namely, the right of use in times of distress."

24. The said passage, be it noted, has been quoted Pratibha Rani V Suraj Kumar and another. In the said case, the majority referred to the stridhan as described in "Hindu Law" by N.R. Raghavachariar and Maine's "Treatise on Hindu Law". The Court after analyzing the classical texts opined that:-

"It is, therefore, manifest that the position of stridhan of a Hindu married woman's property during coverture is absolutely clear and unambiguous; she is the absolute owner of such property and can deal with it in any manner she likes — she may spend the whole of it or give it away at her own pleasure by gift or will without any reference to her husband. Ordinarily, the husband has no right or interest in it with the sole exception that in times of extreme distress, as in famine, illness or the like, the husband can utilize it but he is morally bound to restore it or its value when he is able to do so. It may be further noted that this right is purely personal to the husband and the property so received by him in marriage cannot be proceeded against even in execution of a decree for debt."

25. In the said case, the Court ruled:-

"... a pure and simple entrustment of stridhan without creating any rights in the husband excepting putting the articles in his possession does not entitle him to use the same to the detriment of his wife without her consent. The husband has no justification for not returning the said articles as and when demanded by the wife nor can he burden her with losses of business by using the said property which was never intended by her while entrusting possession of stridhan. On the allegations in the complaint, the husband is no more and no less than a pure and simple custodian acting on behalf of his wife and if he diverts the entrusted property elsewhere or for different purposes he takes a clear risk of prosecution under Section 406 of the IPC. On a parity of reasoning, it is manifest that the husband, being only a custodian of the stridhan of his wife, cannot be said to be in joint possession thereof and thus acquire a joint interest in the property."

26. The decision rendered in the said case was referred for a fresh look by a three-Judge Bench. The three-Judge Bench Rashmi Kumar (smt) V. Mahesh Kumar Bhada while considering the issue in the said case, ruled that :-

"9. A woman's power of disposal, independent of her husband's control, is not confined to saudayika but extends to other properties as well. Devala says: "A woman's maintenance (vritti), ornaments, perquisites (sulka), gains (labha), are her stridhana. She herself has the exclusive right to enjoy it. Her husband has no right to use it except in distress...." In N.R. Raghavachariar's Hindu Law — Principles and Precedents, (8th Edn.) edited by Prof. S. Venkataraman, one of the renowned Professors of Hindu Law para 468 deals with "Definition of Stridhana". In para 469 dealing with "Sources of acquisition" it is stated that the sources of acquisition of property in a woman's possession are: gifts before marriage, wedding gifts, gifts subsequent to marriage etc. Para 470 deals with "Gifts to a maiden". Para 471 deals with "Wedding gifts" and it is stated therein that properties gifted at the time of marriage to the bride, whether by relations or strangers, either Adhiyagni or Adhyavahanika, are the bride's stridhana. In para 481 at page 426, it is stated that ornaments presented to the bride by her husband or father constitute her Stridhana property. In para 487 dealing with "powers during coverture" it is stated that saudayika meaning the gift of affectionate kindred, includes both Yautaka or gifts received at the time of marriage as well as its negative Ayautaka. In respect of such property, whether given by gift or will she be the absolute owner and can deal with it in any way she likes. She may spend, sell or give it away at her own pleasure.

It is thus clear that the properties gifted to her before the marriage, at the time of marriage or at the time of giving farewell or thereafter are her stridhana properties. It is her absolute property with all rights to dispose at her own pleasure. He has no control over her stridhana property. Husband may use it during the time of his distress but nonetheless he has a moral obligation to restore the same or its value to his wife. Therefore, stridhana property does not become a joint property of the wife and the husband and the husband has no title or independent dominion over the property as owner thereof."

After so stating the Court proceeded to rule that stridhana property is the exclusive property of the wife on proof that she entrusted the property or dominion over the stridhana property to her husband or any other member of the family, there is no need to establish any further special agreement to establish that the property was given to the husband or other member of the family. Further, the Court observed that it is always a question of fact in each case as to how the property came to be entrusted to the husband or any other member of the family by the wife when she left the matrimonial home or was driven out therefrom. Thereafter, the Court adverted to the concept of entrustment and eventually concurred with the view in the case of Pratibha Rani. It is necessary to note here that the question had arisen whether it is a continuing offence and limitation could begin to run every day lost its relevance in the said case, for the Court on scrutiny came to hold that the complaint preferred by the complainant for the commission of the criminal breach of trust under Section 406 of the Indian Penal Code was within limitation.

Regard being had to the aforesaid statement of law; we have to see whether retention of stridhan by the husband or any other family members is a continuing offence or not. There can be no dispute that wife can file a suit for realization of the stridhan but it does not debar her to lodge a criminal complaint for criminal breach of trust. We must state that was the situation before the 2005 Act came into force. In the 2005 Act, the definition of "aggrieved person" clearly postulates about the status of any woman who has been subjected to domestic violence as defined under Section 3 of the said Act. "Economic abuse" as it has been defined in Section 3 (iv) of the said Act has a large canvass. Section 12, relevant portion of which have been reproduced hereinbefore, provides for procedure for obtaining orders of reliefs. It has been held in Inderjit Singh Grewal (supra) that Section 498 of the Code of Criminal Procedure applies to the said case under the 2005 Act as envisaged under Section 28 and 32 of the said Act read with Rule 15(6) of the Protection of Women from Domestic Violence Rules, 2006. We need not advert to the same as we are of the considered opinion that as long as the status of the aggrieved person remains and stridhan remains in the custody of the husband, the wife can always put forth her claim under Section 12 of the 2005 Act. We are disposed to think so as the status between the parties is not severed because of the decree of dissolution of marriage. The concept of "continuing offence" gets attracted from the date of deprivation of stridhan, for neither the husband nor any other family members can have any right over the stridhan and they remain the custodians. For the purpose of the 2005 Act, she can submit an application to the Protection Officer for one or more of the reliefs under the 2005 Act.

Maintenance UNDER CRPC 125 and Domestic violence act.

"Cleary the scope of Section 20 of the DV Act is much wider than that of Section 125 Cr.P.C.. While Section 125 Cr.P.C. talks only of maintenance, Section 20 DV Act stipulates payment of monetary relief to meet the expenses incurred and losses suffered as a result of the domestic violence including but not limited to loss of earning, medical expenses, loss caused due to destruction, damage or removal of any property from the control of aggrieved person". It further observed by citing Section-20(1d) of DV Act as *"This clearly shows that an order under Section 20 DV Act is not restricted by an order under section 125 Cr.P.C.. The Trial Court clearly erred in not appreciating the distinction between the two provisions and the reasoning is clouded by an impression that the respondent*

– wife in the application under section 23 was only seeking an order of maintenance, which is not the case. In her application under section 23 of the DV Act, the respondent wife has inter-alia sought residence rights under Section 19 and protection under Section 18 apart from the monetary relief under Section 20".

"Further, it may be seen that proceeding under the DV Act and under section 125 Cr.P.C are independent of each other and have different scope, though there is an overlap. In so far as the overlap is concerned, law has catered for that eventuality and laid down that at the time of consideration of an application for grant of maintenance under DV Act, maintenance fixed under section 125 Cr.P.C shall be taken into account"

Maintenance given in proceedings under Section 125 Cr.P.C. has to be adjusted while computing the maintenance in the proceedings arising out of the Domestic Violence Act, 2005. on a conjoint reading of Sections 20, 26 and 36 of the Domestic Violence Act, was of the opinion: **"the provisions of DV Act dealing with maintenance are supplementary in the provisions of other laws and therefore maintenance can be granted to the aggrieved person(s) under the DV Act which would also be in addition to any order of maintenance arising out of Section 125 of CrPC."** Furthermore, **"On the converse, if any order is passed by the Family Court under Section 24 HMA, the same would not debar the Court in the proceedings arising out of DV Act or proceedings under Section 125 CrPC instituted by the wife/aggrieved person claiming maintenance."**

The Court also clarified: "However, it cannot be laid down as a proposition of law that once an order of maintenance has been passed by any Court then the same cannot be re-adjudicated upon by any other Court. The legislative mandate envisages grant of maintenance to the wife under various statutes such as HMA, Hindu Adoption and Maintenance Act, 1956, Section 125 CrPC as well as Section 20 of DV Act. As such various statutes have been enacted to provide for the maintenance to the wife and it is nowhere the intention of the legislature that once any order is passed in either of the proceedings the intention of the legislature that once any order is passed in either of the proceedings, the said order would debar re-adjudication of the issue of maintenance in any other Court."

It is contended that the ambit of proceedings under Section 12 of the D.V.Act are much wider than mere award of maintenance, however once the order of maintenance is passed either by the Court exercising power under Section 125 Cr.P.C. or by the Court under Section 12 of the D.V.Act, the other Court is to take into account the said order and appropriately pass an order. Learned counsel further submits that there is misapplication of the ratio in Renu Mittal (supra).

Section 20 of the D.V.Act lays down as under:-

"20. Monetary reliefs.--(1) While disposing of an application under sub section (1) of section 12, the Magistrate may direct the respondent to pay monetary relief to meet the expenses incurred and losses suffered by the aggrieved person and any child of the aggrieved person as a result of the domestic violence and such relief may include but is not limited to--

(a) the loss of earnings

(b) the medical expenses

(c) the loss caused due to the destruction, damage, or removal of any property from the control of the aggrieved person; and

(d) the maintenance for the aggrieved person as well as her children, if any, including an order under or in addition to an order of maintenance under Section 125 of the Code of Criminal Procedure, 1973 (2 of 1974) or any other law for the time being in force.............."

Reading of Section 20 (1)(d) of the D.V.Act, shows that a Court, which is considering an application under Section 12 of the D.V.Act, would take into account an order of maintenance passed under Section 125 Cr.P.C. or any other law, for the time being, in force.

Reading of Section 2(1)(d) of the D.V.Act further shows that the two proceedings are independent of each other and have different scope, though there is an overlap. Insofar as the overlap is concerned, law has catered for that eventuality and laid down that at the time of consideration of an application for grant of maintenance under Section 12 of the D.V.Act, the maintenance fixed under Section 125 Cr.P.C. shall be taken into account.

Pendency of proceedings under Section 12 of the D.V.Act do not act as an embargo for consideration of an application under section 125 Cr.P.C. Rather, it implies that both the proceedings can continue simultaneously. It is only when there is a determination of maintenance under Section 125 Cr.P.C., that the order would become a relevant factor to be taken into account by the court considering grant of maintenance under Section 12 of the D.V.Act.

The mere fact that two proceedings are initiated by a party; one under Section 125 Cr.P.C. and another under Section 12 of the Act does not imply that one of the two has to be adjourned.

It may also be noticed that the proceedings under the D.V.Act are not only confined to award of maintenance but several other monetary reliefs inter alia expenses incurred, losses suffered, loss of earnings, medical expenses, loss caused due to destruction, damage or removal of any property maintenance etc.

There is thus clearly a distinction between the scope and power exercised by the Magistrate under Section 125 Cr.P.C. and under Section 12 of the D.V.Act.

CHAPTER 10

TRANSFER OF DIVORCE PETITION.

CAN A WIFE GET TRANSFERRED DIVORCE PETITION TO A PLACE WHERE SHE RESIDES?

Yes, she can file a transfer petition to get the divorce Petition transferred to her place but the court has the power to decide the same.

Transfer of cases relating to Matrimonial Disputes from a court situated in a particular state to a court situated in another state, can only be done by the way of Transfer Petition which may be filed by either party to the case before Hon'ble Supreme Court of India. Such Transfer Petition is filed under Section 25 of Code of Civil Procedure, wherein under the said provision, Supreme Court of India has original Jurisdiction to transfer a civil case relating to Matrimonial Dispute, based on facts of the case, & circumstances of parties, and if such transfer is expedient for ends of Justice. Similar power may be exercised by High courts in the event transfer of case is sought from one district to another within one state, over which the concerned High Court has Jurisdiction.

Section 25 is based on the 'doctrine of forum convenience' which means –'the best forum' where a fair trial can be held. Normally it is presumed that if petitioner has filed a case before a particular court having jurisdiction – it is the best forum. The burden is on the person seeking transfer of case, to prove that if the proceedings are not transferred, he/she would suffer irreparable injustice, on the merits of the case (i.e. going unrepresented in the case) and/or with issues respect to personal life (i.e. loss of job/health/ safety issues). The party seeking Transfer would also have to prove that the latter is irreparable in monetary terms. Once party to the case who has filed Transfer Petition is able to prove as mentioned above, he/she would also have to prove that he/she will not suffer similar losses if the proceedings are transferred. Hence it is a double burden of proof for the party seeking Transfer of case. If party to the case succeeds in proving as mentioned above, the balance of convenience is said to lie in favour of concerned party to the case, who has sought Transfer of case. In such cases Courts are usually inclined in favour of Women.

Usually Divorce cases, and cases related to custody of children, & case of Civil Nature can be transferred by Supreme Court, when Transfer Petition is filed under Section 25 of Civil Procedure Code.

CHAPTER NO

CHAPTER 11

FOREIGN DECREE OF DIVORCE

Foreign Decree of Divorce

Many times, there comes a question "how good is a decree of divorce granted by a foreign court with regard to a Hindu couple married in India?"

The foremost answer that would surface with us would be, that, the Hindu couple residing/working in a foreign land ought to be governed by the matrimonial laws in force at that place. As a corollary, the decree of divorce granted by the foreign court should be valid.

However, Section 1 of the Hindu Marriage Act, 1955 which reads thus:

1. *Short title and extent*—(1) This Act may be called the Hindu Marriage Act, 1955.

(2) It extends to the whole of India except the State of Jammu and Kashmir and applies also to Hindus domiciled in the territories to which this Act extends who are outside the said territories.

It is for this reason that Hindus married as per Hindu Rights in India, although settled abroad, are primarily required by law to process divorce proceedings only as per the said Act i.e. applying the Hindu Marriage Act, 1955.

Under section 13 of the Hindu Marriage Act, 1955 the grounds are mentioned under which divorce can be granted. The said Section mentions that divorce can be taken exclusively on the stated grounds. When the grounds have been specifically stated, it excludes the scope of granting divorce on any other ground. Few grounds mentioned in the said Act are as follows:

(*i*) petitioner has been treated with cruelty.

(*ii*) petitioner has been deserted.

(*iii*) respondent has ceased to be a Hindu; and

(*iv*) respondent has been of an incurable unsound mind.

To complete the narration of codified law on the subject, reference to Section 13 of the Code of Civil Procedure, 1908 is essential which reads as under:

> 13. *When foreign judgment not conclusive* — A foreign judgment shall be conclusive as to any matter thereby directly adjudicated upon between the same parties or between parties under whom they or any of them claim litigating under the same title except—
>
> (*a*) where it has not been pronounced by a court of competent jurisdiction.
>
> (*b*) where it has not been given on the merits of the case.
>
> (*c*) where it appears on the face of the pro-

ceedings to be founded on an incorrect view of international law or a refusal to recognize the law of India in cases in which such law is applicable.

(*d*) where the proceedings in which the judgment was obtained are opposed to natural justice.

(*e*) where it has been obtained by fraud; and

(*f*) where it sustains a claim founded on a breach of any law in force in India.

The Supreme Court of India in *Y. Narasimha Rao v. Y. Venkata Lakshmi*. This Court ruled that:

(*a*) Court of competent jurisdiction would be the one which the law under which parties are married, recognizes. Any other court would be court without jurisdiction, unless both parties voluntarily and unconditionally subject themselves to the jurisdiction of that Court.

(*b*) It was held that the decision must be given on the "merits" of the case i.e.:

(*i*) The ground of divorce in the decision of the foreign court should be a ground available under the Hindu Marriage Act, 1955. For instance, if the ground of the foreign decree was cruelty on the applicant, this would be acceptable, as "cruelty" is a stated ground under the Hindu Marriage Act, 1955. But the same cannot be said for "irretrievable breakdown of marriage", as this is not a ground under the Hindu Marriage Act, 1955.

(*ii*) The decision should be a result of contest between the parties. The non-applicant should have unconditionally submitted to the jurisdiction of the foreign court and contested the claim or agreed to the passing of the decree. The concept of acquiescence to jurisdiction would not suffice.

(*c*) Refusal to recognize the law of India, is covered by

saying that the ground for divorce in the foreign decree is a ground available under the Hindu Marriage Act, 1955.

(*d*) The foreign judgment was obtained as opposed to natural justice. The concept of natural justice is the provision of fair hearing; absence of bias of Judge and following the elementary principles of fair play. This is a larger concept but shortly can be stated as essential trappings in order to have a fair adjudication. Where for instance respondent was denied documents filed by the other side or where the respondent was denied the opportunity to cross-examine witnesses of the other side, without a justifiable cause, these would be opposed to the principles of natural justice.

(*e*) Where the foreign decree was obtained by fraud. Fraud at any stage vitiates legal proceedings. It is often said that law and fraud cannot co-exist.

In *Satya v. Teja Singh* when the respondent had instituted a foreign court proceeding, in a court in whose jurisdiction the applicant has never lived, respondent had made a false representation that respondent was a bona fide resident of that State. It was held that the respondent had practiced fraud on the foreign court by concealing this fact. Therefore, that foreign court had no territorial jurisdiction. That foreign court decree was declared invalid by the Supreme Court of India.

Briefly, the expression "where it has not been given on merits of the case" was commented upon by the Supreme Court of India in *International Woollen Mills* v. *Standard Wool (UK) Ltd.* The view taken was when evidence was led by the plaintiff applicant in the foreign court, even though the opposite side may have been served but not appearing, the decision would be "on merits". This Court concurred with the law laid down in another case which stated that:

A decision on the merits involves the application of the mind of the Court to the truth or falsity of the plaintiff's case and therefore though a judgment passed after a judicial consideration of the matter by taking evidence may be a decision on the merits even though passed ex parte, a decision passed without evidence of any kind but passed only on his pleadings cannot be held to be a decision on the merits.

ISSUES BEFORE THE INDIAN COURTS

Indian courts were confronted with situations wherein Hindu couples married in India as per Hindu Law, settled in a foreign land, develop matrimonial disputes, and approach a foreign court. This situation demanded the Indian courts to determine whether the decrees passed by the foreign court as a consequence of the matrimonial disputes between the Hindu couples settled abroad, had any efficacy in India.

Concept of "Comity of Courts"

This is a view taken by the courts, which is known as the concept of "comity of courts". This means that courts in various countries grant probity to decrees of foreign courts. The understanding being, the courts all over the world adjudicate the rights of the parties and therefore, show mutual respect. This principle was approved by the Supreme Court of India in *Elizabeth Dinshaw v. Arvand M. Dinshaw*. The Court recorded the observation that:

9. ... it is the duty of all courts in all countries to do all they can to ensure that the wrongdoer does not gain an advantage by his wrongdoing.

The courts in all countries ought, as I see it, to be careful not to do anything to encourage this tendency. This substitution of self-help for due process of law in this field can only harm the interests of wards generally, and a Judge should, as I see it, pay regard to the orders of the proper foreign court unless he is satisfied beyond reasonable doubt that to do so would inflict serious harm on the child.

The Supreme Court of India in another case *Alcon Electronics (P) Ltd. v. Celem SA of FOS 34320 Roujan*, recorded the following:

The principles of comity of nation demand us to respect the order of English Court. Even in regard to an interlocutory order, Indian courts have to give due weight to such order unless it falls under any of the exceptions under Section 13 CPC. These are the competing considerations before the Indian courts. That is the codified laws and the concept of "comity of courts". These have to be reconciled by the Indian courts. In a different context, namely, custody of child, in an inter-country dispute, Supreme Court of India had occasioned to opine in *Ruchi Majoo v. Sanjeev Majoo*. It may be clarified that custody of child matter is to be viewed completely differently as against dissolution of marriage. This is for the reason that in custody of child matters, welfare of the child is of paramount consideration by the Court. Supreme Court of India took the view that: Recognition of decrees and orders passed by foreign courts remains an eternal dilemma inasmuch as whenever called upon to do so, courts in this country are bound to determine the validity of such decrees and orders keeping in view the provisions of Section 13 CPC. Simply because a foreign court has taken a particular view on any aspect concerning the welfare of the minor is not enough for the courts in this country to shut out an independent consideration of the matter. Judicial pronouncements on the subject are not on virgin ground. Since no system of private international law exists that can claim universal recognition on this issue, Indian courts have to decide the issue regarding the validity of the decree in accordance with the Indian law. Comity of courts simply demands consideration of any such order issued by foreign courts and not necessarily their enforcement.

In that context, Supreme Court of India in *Prateek Gupta v. Shilpi Gupta,* balanced the foreign court order on custody by holding that it is one of the relevant factors without getting fixated therewith. Court held that:

while examining the question on merits, would bear in mind the welfare of the child as of paramount and predominant importance while noting the pre-existing order of the foreign court, if any, as only one of the factors and not get fixated therewith.

A different situation arose before the Delhi High Court in *Harmeeta Singh v. Rajat Taneja.* Here the husband had filed proceedings in the foreign court. Wife has approached the Delhi High Court by way of a civil suit. High Court restrained the husband for continuing with the proceedings in the foreign court, as the wife had no spouse visa, she possibly could not defend the proceeding in the foreign court. Of course, there was no occasion for the wife to submit to jurisdiction of the foreign court.

Broadly Two Categories of Cases

Two categories of cases can be carved out on the basis whether the opposite party in the foreign court appeared and actively participated or not. Therefore, the subject can be easily stated under the following two heads:

(i) Did Not Attend Nor Actively Participated

The non-applicant always has an option not to attend nor actively participate in the foreign court proceedings. This would be taken as; the non-applicant did not submit to the jurisdiction of the foreign court. This, however, does not mean that the non-applicant is not even required to be served in the foreign court proceedings. Non-service would amount to denial of opportunity to be heard.

As the non-applicant did not submit to the jurisdiction, it is further said that this non-applicant did not chance a judgment in his/her favour. Challenge to the foreign court decree in such a situation may be entertained by the Indian courts. It cannot, therefore, be said that having participated, having submitted to the jurisdiction and having made submissions before the foreign court, now because the verdict of the foreign court is against the non-applicant, he is now challenging the same in the Indian court.

The non-applicant must be served with notice of the foreign court proceedings. Or else, the proceedings would be taken in law to be a nullity i.e. of no value in law. If this is a situation, Indian courts are likely to declare the entire foreign court proceedings as void.

(ii) Did Attend And Actively Participated
This question automatically answers itself, when contrasted with the above answer. Having attended and having participated, the non-applicant (respondent) in the foreign court cannot complain that he/she was not heard if the respondent had voluntarily submitted to the jurisdiction of the foreign court. The respondent is free to make an alternative plea under the jurisdiction of the foreign court for grant of alimony or monthly maintenance. To adjudicate the same, the foreign court would be free to follow laws laid by its

own land.

Another form of "attend and actively participate" is when the non-applicant consents to the passing of the decree of divorce.

Consequences of a Foreign Decree of Divorce Being Held as Invalid

Respondent cannot sit with the comfort that he/she has a decree for divorce from a foreign court. Consequences may appear soon thereafter or maybe years later. The other side may apply for its cancellation in the Indian court. In such an eventuality if:

(*i*) The respondent remarries, he may be prosecuted for bigamy. Case in point is *Y. Narasimha Rao v. Y. Venkata Lakshmi.*

(*ii*) Opposite party may file for maintenance.

(*iii*) Issue of custody of children can be raised.

Executability of Foreign Court Decree

This is contained in Section 44-A CPC read with Section 13 CPC. Although Section 44-A CPC is couched in general phraseology and would seem to apply to the execution of foreign decrees in general. However, when it comes to specific laws i.e. the Hindu Marriage Act, 1955 or the issue of custody of the child, Section 44-A seems to have little application.

These specific Acts have an overbearing effect on Section 44-A CPC. This is clear from sub-section (3) of Section 44-A which makes it clear that this is subject to the decree falling in any of the exceptions contained in Section 13 CPC.

Conclusion

The above discussion only shows how complicated the position is regarding the validity of a foreign court decree of divorce. It can perhaps be stated that a Hindu couple married in India would be well advised to seek a divorce from an Indian court only. There can be little comfort from the fact that the foreign court decree was passed and some time has elapsed or that there is inaction of the opposite side. Consequences may appear several years later.

THE NEXT STEP

The process of simplification could begin for instance from a Hindu couple permanently settled abroad. If facts show that they were indeed permanently settled in the foreign land, then, such a couple could be said to have causal and most immediate territorial connection with the foreign land. It could be held that their court of competent jurisdiction could be foreign court and their proper law i.e. codified law would be the foreign law. This is stated on the strength of principles given by the Supreme Court of India in *Surinder Kaur Sandhu* v. *Harbax Singh Sandhu*:

The modern theory of conflict of laws recognizes and, in any event, prefers the jurisdiction of the State which has the most intimate contact with the issues arising in the case, Ordinarily, jurisdiction must follow upon functional lines. That is to say, for example, that in matters relating to matrimony and custody, the law of that place must govern which has the closest concern with the well-being of the spouses and the welfare of the offspring of marriage.

By adopting this approach, a practical way may appear for couples settled abroad. They may not need to have recourse to Indian courts. The development of law could march in this direction.

Therefore, foreign court has no jurisdiction to entertain the petition according to the concerned Indian Act under which admittedly the parties were married. However, the relevant provisions of Section 13 of the Code of Civil Procedure, 1908 (Code) are capable of being interpreted foreign court judgment with its own six pillars. Under Section 13 of the Code, a foreign judgment is not conclusive as to any matter thereby "directly adjudicated upon" "between the parties" if: (a) it has not been pronounced by a Court of competent jurisdiction; or (b) it has not been given on the merits of the case; or (c) it is founded on an incorrect view of international law or a refusal to recognize the law of India in cases in which such law is applicable; or (d) the proceedings are opposed to natural justice, or (e) it is obtained by fraud, or (f) it sustains a claim founded on a breach of any law in force in India. It is thus clear that in order to make a foreign judgment conclusive in India; it must be shown that it complies with all the above mentioned six conditions. There is no compliance of any one of these conditions; then, foreign judgment will not be conclusive and consequently not legally effective and binding in India. A decree of a foreign Court is normally recognised by a Court in another jurisdiction as a matter of comity and public policy. But no country is bound to recognise and give effect to a decree of a foreign Court if it is repugnant to its own laws and public policy. So far as India is concerned, a judgment of a foreign Court creates estoppel or resjudicata between the same parties provided such judgment is not subject to attack under any of the Clauses (a) to (f) of section 13 of the Code. FOREIGN MUTUAL CONSENT DIVORCE, if parties obtained divorce by mutual consent and therefore the courts of India do not want to interfere with it. Since either party obtained divorce through mutual consent from any foreign country it implies that your ex

spouse participated in the divorce proceedings. So, he/she cannot now challenge the judgment of foreign court in an Indian court. The judgment of foreign court is final. There is no requirement of any validation of your divorce from an Indian court. As a corollary thereto, you are free to remarry. The well-accepted universal principle of law can be stated as – If someone has accepted the authority of a court, it cannot be open to the person to later question the authority of the court.

The Supreme Court has stated as follows:

If marriage solemnized of any Indian law, (a) the foreign court that grants divorce must be acceptable under provision of concerned personal or civil statute; and (b) the foreign court should grant divorce only on the grounds which are permissible under provision of concerned personal or civil statute. The two conditions make it almost impossible to get a legally valid divorce from a foreign court since no foreign court is an acceptable one provision of concerned personal or civil statute of India and also because no foreign court is likely to consider the provisions of concerned personal or civil statute of India before granting divorce.

EXCEPTION OF THE VERDICT

A. Men and women must be domiciled and permanently resident of that foreign land and the foreign court should decide the case based on concerned personal or civil statute of India

B. Both parties voluntarily and effectively attend the court proceedings and contests the claim on grounds of divorce as permitted under the provisions of concerned personal or civil statute of India.

C. Mutual consents to grant of divorce DIVORCE – ATTENDING PROCEEDINGS.

Both parties contesting the divorce actively attends the divorce proceedings in the foreign court, the chances of either parties able to later successfully approach Indian courts against an unfavourable judgment of the foreign court are very low. Indian courts, or for that matters courts anywhere in the world, do not wish to encourage court- mocking. The well-accepted universal principle of law can be stated as – If someone has accepted the authority of a court, it cannot be open to the person to later question the authority of the court.

CONSEQUENCES OF INVALID DECREE OF DIVORCE

If a man has obtained divorce decree from foreign court without proper ways:- 1. If he remarries, he may be prosecuted for bigamy. 2. Wife (divorced as per foreign law) may file for maintenance.

3. In case the man dies without making a will, the first wife will have the right to her share in the property of the man while the second wife will get nothing because her marriage will not be considered legitimate. If a woman has obtained divorce decree from foreign court without proper ways:- If she remarries, her new husband may be prosecuted under section 497 of Indian Penal Code under which he may face imprisonment of five years. The wife will, of course, be liable for punishment under section 494 of Indian Penal Code for bigamy.

SUGGESTIVE SOLUTIONS: If marriage was solemnized under Indian custom or Indian statute, then it is better to seek solution for divorce through Indian court alone. Foreign decree of divorce is valid in India as following two aspects A. When the couple decides to take divorce by mutual consent and B. When the person who is contesting divorce attends divorce proceedings and the foreign court grants divorce on grounds that are permitted grounds of provisions of concerned personal or civil statute of India. Divorce is a process by which the marriage between two adults comes to an end which may be solemnized under different laws like Hindus which includes Sikhs, Jains, Buddhists are governed by the Hindu Marriage Act,1955 while Christians are governed by Indian Divorce Act, 1869 and the Indian Christian Marriage Act,1872.

The Muslims are governed by Personnel laws of Divorce and also the Dissolution of Marriage Act,1939 and the Muslim Women (Protection of Rights on Divorce) Act,1986. Similarly, Parsis are governed by Parsi Marriage & Divorce Act-1936. Apart from the above laws, other marriages are governed by the Special Marriage Act,1954.

CHAPTER NO 12

MUTUAL CONSENT DIVORCE UNDER
13 B OF HINDU MARRIAGE ACT.

Under Section 13B(1), a divorce petition can be moved by a couple following a separation of one year. This may be followed by another six months of waiting period under Section 13B(2) for getting a decree.   Supreme Court in Amardeep Singh v. Harveen Kaur (2017) 8 SCC 746 has stated that provision of Section 13B(2) is not mandatory but directory. Apex Court has stated that, the courts can grant divorce after waiving of six months' waiting period on being satisfied that the "waiting period will only prolong their agony" and that all efforts of conciliation have been futile. The courts, waiving of the cooling off period will also consider whether the estranged couple has settled all differences relating to alimony, custody of children etc.

Section 14 provides that no petition for divorce to be presented within one year of marriage provided that the Court may, upon application made to it in accordance with such rules as may be made by the High Court in that behalf, allow a petition to be presented (before one year has elapsed) since the date of the marriage on the ground that the case is one of exceptional hardship to the petitioner or of exceptional depravity on the part of the respondent. The Divorce Proceedings can take place by adopting two procedures which are as follows:

- she can file for contested divorce under section 13 and if she is able to get a maintenance order etc. and also filing of domestic violence, maintenance petition or application then it will to some extend make the husband agree to come forward for some settlement which naturally ends in mutual consent divorce or it is settled through meditation. Further if the husband does not come forward for compromise then the wife has to prove at least one ground of divorce which can be done by producing evidence of herself, oral, documentary or circumstantial evidence, supported with other witnesses who whose evidence can help in proving ground of divorce, if the ground is in respect of mental disorder or husband suffering from venereal disease then medical documents and expert evidence of doctors is a must to prove such grounds. Mutual Divorce is a legal process of separation, when both the husband and wife want to separate with their own will after marriage, is called at Divorce with Mutual Consent. Both husband and wife can apply for the divorce by mutual consent.

The Procedure for Filing for Mutual Divorce:

Important Issues to be Settled before Proceeding:

1. Child Custody: Which partner will get the child custody after divorce

2. Alimony/Maintenance: If one of the partner is unable to meet his daily expenses then other needs to pay him a certain sum of amount as alimony (one-time settlement or monthly payment). It is subject to mutual understanding between the partners (husband and wife).

3. Settlement of Property and Assets: Settling the ownership rights of property and asset like dwelling house, bank accounts, movable assets between the parties (Husband and wife)

Requirement of Documents for filing Mutual Divorce Petition:

1. Marriage Certificate or wedding card

2. Address Proof - Husband and Wife. Aadhaar card, passport etc

3. Four Photographs of Marriage.

4. Identity card photographs of both husband and wife

5. Details of profession and Income (Salary slips, appointment letter)

6. Details of Property and Asset owned

7. Information about family (husband and wife)

8. Evidence of Staying separately for an year or above

9. Evidence relating to the failed attempts of reconciliation

· **Where can the Mutual Divorce Petition be filed?**

· Where the couple was last residing as husband and wife,

· Where the husband or wife is presently residing.

· Where the marriage was solemnized

Procedure to Dissolve the Marriage by Mutual Consent:

Step 1: Filing of the Petition in the Family Court

Joint petition for dissolution of marriage for a decree of divorce is presented to the Family Court by both the spouses on the ground stating that they have not been able to reconcile the differences and live together. Thus, have mutually agreed to dissolve the marriage and they have been living separately for a period of one year or more. This petition has to be signed by both the parties.

Step 2: Appearance before the Family Court Judge for First Motion for Divorce

Both the parties will enter their appearance in the Court along with their legal counsels. Family Court Judge will go through the contents of the petition along with all the documents presented in the Court. Court may attempt to reconcile the differences between the spouses, however, if this is not possible, the matter proceeds further.

Step 3: Statement on Oath or Mediation report.

After going through the contents of the application, Court may order the party's statements to be recorded on oath and then pass a divorce decree or the matter is sent the parties to mediation where the settlement is recorded through mediation who will also make efforts to unite the couple and reduce the terms of settlement in writing and report the settlement and thereafter the court verifies the report and court passes the decree based on the report filed by mediator after making due enquiry whether they accept the terms of settlement and then pass a decree of divorce if 6 months is completed from date of filing of Petition or if the court has waived the 6 months waiting period on application filed by the parties.

Step 4: Hearing & Final Decree of Divorce

If the court is satisfied after hearing the parties that the contents in the petition are true and that there cannot be any possibility of reconciliation and cohabitation and the issues pertaining to alimony, custody of children, properties etc. are settled, Court can pass a decree of divorce declaring the marriage to be dissolved.

Divorce becomes final once the decree of divorce has been passed by the court. The ultimate suggest for a wife to get divorce is that firstly if the divorce is possible through mutual consent divorce then go with mutual consent divorce which is easy and with the recent decision of supreme court, if the concerned court waives the waiting period of 6 months by allowing the application then divorce can get obtained within vey few days or couple of months, if husband is not ready for divorce and if the wife is unable to maintain herself or is subjected to domestic violence or cruelty.

In nut shall if it is contested divorce and if some maintenance and protection orders are received the husband is most likely to agree to pay permanent alimony and divorce, if not then wife has to prove grounds of divorce by her evidence, supported by other oral, documentary and other witnesses, expert evidence supported by recent Judgements of supreme court and high courts. Further in order to make it more easy it is necessary to provide all the details of married life, all property documents, income proof documents, loan documents, medical health issue documents, all minute details as far as possible with date, time and circumstances, and more the details are provided to the lawyer, the lawyer will be able to present the case more effectively and correctly supported by documents and oral evidence of wife and other witnesses before the court and which in turn make it easy for the court too to pass judgement in your favour as it is supported by evidence and judgment of supreme court and high court. So, provide, Complete details to your Advocate who will in turn draft your petition in a systematic and organized manner.

DISCLAIMER CLAUSE

THE CONTENTS OF THIS BOOK ARE PROVIDED FOR GENERAL INFORMATIONAL PURPOSES ONLY THEY DO NOT CONSTITUTE LEGAL ADVICE OR A LEGAL OPINION ON ANY SPECIFIC FACTS OR CIRCUMSTANCES. YOU ARE URGED TO TAKE YOUR OWN DECISIONS CONCERNING YOUR SITUATION AND SPECIFIC LEGAL QUESTIONS YOU MAY HAVE. THE AUTHOR OR THE PUBLISHER IS IN NO WAY RESPONSIBLE FOR ANY ACTION TAKEN ON BASIS OF INFORMATION PROVIDED IN THIS BOOK. THIS BOOK IS ONLY FOR INFORMATION AND NO ATTORNEY CLI-

ENT RELATIONSHIP IS ESTABLISHED
AUTHOR:BHARAT NARASGOUDA

www.ingramcontent.com/pod-product-compliance
Lightning Source LLC
Chambersburg PA
CBHW052033150726